CHECKLIST OF FLOWERING PLANTS AND FERNS IN THE ISLES OF SCILLY

Rosemary Parslow

Isles of Scilly Museum Publication

2009

CHECKLIST OF FLOWERING PLANTS AND FERNS IN THE ISLES OF SCILLY

INTRODUCTION TO THE THIRD EDITION

The original Museum Check-list compiled by J. Edward Lousley was published in 1975, and revised by Clare Harvey in 1983. Both lists were based on Lousley's 1971 Flora of the Isles of Scilly which is now out of print. Since then there have been many changes in the distribution, frequency and even of species of plants on the islands.

This third checklist is based on records in the database maintained by the author as Botanical Society of the British Isles (BSBI) recorder for the Isles of Scilly. It is hoped to eventually produce an updated, dot-map Flora for Scilly based on those records acquired since c1985 when the author suceeded Clare Harvey as vice-county recorder. The scientific names and order of this checklist are based on Stace, C. (1997) *New Flora of the British Isles*. Cambridge University Press. To save space authors' names have been omitted.

The flora of the Isles of Scilly is unique; many Scillonian plants are of Lusitanian or Mediterranean origin. Some species, orange birdsfoot *Ornithopus pinnatus*, least adderstongue fern *Ophioglossum lusitanicum*, dwarf pansy *Viola kitaibeliana* are not found on mainland Britain. Others such as small-flowered catchfly *Silene gallica*, four-leaved allseed *Polycarpon tetraphyllum*, small-flowered tree-mallow *Lavatera cretica* and early meadowgrass *Poa infirma* are found in Cornwall and elsewhere but nowhere as abundant as they are in the Isles of Scilly. Exceptionally all three taxa of *Ophioglossum* ferns have been recorded on just one island in Scilly - St Agnes.

Many garden escapes and alien introductions have become established on Scilly due to the mildness of the climate. Some of these may be found on uninhabited islands as the result of gull activity – although most do not survive for very long. Yet other plants that are common on the mainland are rare or absent from the Isles of Scilly; examples are coltsfoot *Tussilago farfara*, betony *Stachys officinalis* and even meadow buttercup *Ranunculus acris*.

1

No attempt has been made to distinguish between native or alien plants in this list. Any plant that may be found growing 'wild' is included although some garden
escapes may have been omitted if they are not clearly established away from cultivation. But in time this may change.

There is no one book that includes illustrations or descriptions of all the plant species that occur in Scilly, but as well as Stace (see above) the following are recommended:

Rose, F. (revised by C. O'Reilly) (2006) *The Wild Flower Key*. Warne.
Murphy, R.J., Page, C.N. & Parslow, R.E. in prep. *Ferns and Fern Allies of Cornwall and the Isles of Scilly*.
Murphy, R.J. 2009. Furnitories of Britain and Ireland. BSBI Handbook No 12. Botanical Society of the British Isles.
Blamey, M., Fitter, R. & Fitter, A. (2003) *Wild Flowers of Britain and Ireland*. A&C Black, London.
Sterry, P. 2006 Complete British Wild flowers. Collins.
(The last two include illustrations of some Scilly specialities)

I am grateful to the many people have already contributed records to the database. Although there is not the space to acknowledge individuals here they will all be mentioned when the new Flora is published.

The author would welcome records of plants, especially from new localities or of new species. *But please do not trespass on farms or private land*. Records should include date, locality (ideally with a 6 or 8-figure grid reference) and if the identity needs confirmation a photograph (digital photographs are very useful), drawing or a 'voucher specimen'. Voucher specimens can be essential to confirm an identity and need only be a representative piece of the plant (including a floret, fruit & leaf etc). Please do not send a whole plant if there is only one or very few; a small specimen usually suffices. The author is also willing to identify plants by post; the specimen should be placed in a plastic bag inside a padded envelope and sent first class post with relevant details as above.

Records or specimens should be sent to Rosemary Parslow, 17 St Michael's Road, Ponsanooth, Truro, TR3 7ED. rparslow@cix.co.uk

PTERIDOPHYTA

SELAGINELLACEAE

Selaginella kraussiana Selaginella
Rare. Weed in Tresco Abbey Gardens.

EQUISETACEAE

Equisetum arvense Field horsetail
Rare. Arable fields St Mary's.

PTEROPSIDA - FERNS

OPHIOGLOSSACEAE

Ophioglossum vulgatum Adder's-tongue
Rare. Although a common fern on the mainland, it is only reliably known from one site near Browarth on St Agnes where it grew under bracken until the mid 1990s.

Ophioglossum azoricum Small or Lesser Adder's-tongue
Occasional/locally frequent. Found on heathland, maritime grassland and in bracken fields on all the inhabited islands. Appears to have been lost from a number of former sites. Taller fronds may be mistaken for *O. vulgatum.*

Ophioglossum lusitanicum Early or Least Adder's-tongue
Rare. Only found on Wingletang Down on St Agnes where it is confined to areas of very shallow soil over granite. Appears in late autumn, producing spores in December to January and dying down by spring (may be confused with *O.azoricum* where they grow together, as the emerging tips of *O.azoricum* fronds appear just as *O. lusitanicum* is going over).

Botrychium lunaria Moonwort
Rare. A record from Tresco in 2007 is the first occurrence since 1980 when it was last recorded in dunes at Bar Point, St Mary's.

OSMUNDACEAE

Osmunda regalis Royal fern
Locally frequent. Found in wet areas on both St Mary's and Tresco. On St
Mary's it occurs on both Lower and Higher Moors. On both Tresco and St
Mary's it also occurs among willow carr and along ditch sides, water-filled
pits on heathland and in freshwater seepages at the base of cliffs.

ADIANTACEAE

Adiantum capillus-veneris Maidenhair Fern
Rare. Extinct as native, but occasionally occurs as an escape from cultivation,
recently found on a wall in Hugh Town.

PTERIDACEAE

Pteris cretica
Alien, naturalised in woodland on Tresco.

POLYPODIACEAE

Polypodium agg. Polypody
Frequent. Most records of polypody from Scilly have not separated the taxa.
Recorded from all the inhabited islands as well as Samson and Great Ganilly.

Polypodium interjectum Intermediate Polypody
Frequent. This is the common polypody in Scilly.

Polypodiun vulgare Polypody
Occasional. Records for this species in Scilly have only recently been
separated from those of *P. interjectum*.

Phymatosorus diversifolius Kangaroo Fern
Alien. Damp places around Tresco Abbey

DICKSONIACEAE

Dicksonia antarctica **Australian tree-fern**
Alien. A few sporlings have been found in woodland on Tresco outside the Gardens.

DENNSTAEDTIACEAE

Pteridium aquilinum **Bracken**
Abundant/locally dominant. Very common on both inhabited and all the larger uninhabited islands.

ASPLENIACEAE

Phyllitus scolopendrium **Hart's-tongue Fern**
Locally frequent. Currently found on all the inhabited islands except Bryher. Also recorded from Teän.

Asplenium adiantum-nigrum **Black Spleenwort**
Locally frequent. Probably more common than formerly, apparently having spread since Lousley's time. Recorded from all the inhabited islands, plus Samson, St Helen's and Great Ganilly.

Asplenium x *sarniensis*
Rare. Only one specimen of this rare hybrid between *A.adiantum-nigrum and A. obovatum lanceolatum* is/was known from a site on St Mary's where it appears to have died (2008).

Asplenium marinum **Sea Spleenwort**
Frequent. All inhabited and most uninhabited islands. Predominately coastal but small plants are frequently found inland, including on walls in Hugh Town.

Asplenium obovatum **ssp** *lanceolatum* **Lanceolate Spleenwort**
Locally frequent. Found on walls mainly on St Agnes and St Mary's with a few records from Tresco, St Helen's and formerly Samson.

Asplenium ruta-muraria **Wall-rue**
Rare. Only known from one site on a garden wall on St Mary's and on a building on St Martin's.

Maidenhair Spleenwort *Asplenium trichomanes quadrivalens*
Rare. Found on walls on St Martin's (although the best display on a wall in Higher Town was lost when the wall was repointed). Other records from Tresco, St Agnes & St Mary's are mainly associated with old greenhouses and other buildings.

Ceterach officinarum **Rustyback Fern**
Extinct. Last recorded 1992. Formerly known from a barn wall on St Martin's; but lost during repointing when the barn was converted to a house.

WOODSIACEAE

Athyrium filix-femina **Lady Fern**
Locally frequent. Widespread in wetland sites on St Mary's and Tresco.

DRYOPTERIDACEAE

Polystichum setiferum **Soft Shield Fern**
Occasional. There are scattered records from St Agnes, St Mary's, Tresco and St Martin's. Also known from Samson, Teän and Northwethel.

Cyrtomium falcatum **House Holly Fern**
Occasional. Established alien in several places on St Mary's.

Dryopteris affinis **Scaly Male Fern**
Rare. Tresco and St Mary's. This, and the subspecies *affinus* and *borreri* are almost certainly under-recorded.

Dryopteris carthusiana **Narrow Buckler fern**
Rare. Only recorded from St Mary's.

Dryopteris dilatata **Broad Buckler fern**
Locally frequent. Only well recorded from St Mary's, with a scatter of records from the other inhabited islands. Also found on Teän and Samson.

Dryopteris filix-mas Male Fern
Frequent. Found on all the inhabited islands other than Bryher from where it appears to be absent. Also found on Samson and Teän.

BLECHNACEAE

Woodwardia radicans
 Alien, recorded on Tresco.

Blechnum cordatum Chilean Hard Fern
Occasional. Alien recorded on Tresco and St Mary's. Was found on Ragged Island in Eastern Isles in 1987.

Blechnum spicant Hard Fern
Rare. St Mary's and Tresco. Apparently declining.

AZOLLACEAE

Azolla filiculoides Water Fern
Occasional. Established alien on water bodies on St Mary's and Tresco. A pernicious and invasive plant of freshwater sites, frequently completely covering the water surface.

Atriplex lacinata

PINOPSIDA - CONIFERS

PINACEAE

***Pinus radiata* Monterey Pine**
Locally frequent. Planted on the inhabited islands, seedlings are uncommon.

***Pinus contorta* Lodgepole Pine**
Locally frequent. Planted as windbreak on the inhabited islands.

[*Pinus pinaster* Maritime pine
St Agnes – needs confirmation]

CUPRESSACEAE
***Cupressus macrocarpa* Monterey Cypress**
Occasional. Planted on the inhabited islands.

Eryngium maritimum

MAGNOLIIDAE - DICOTYLEDONS

RANUNCULACEAE

***Caltha palustris* Marsh Marigold**
Rare. Garden introduction to pools on Tresco and St Mary's.

***Clematis vitalba* Traveller's Joy**
Rare. Probable garden escape St Mary's.

***Ranunculus repens* Creeping buttercup**
Abundant. All the inhabited islands; also recorded from St Helen's, Great Ganilly and Samson. Plants along the Holy Vale stream can be unusually large.

***Ranunculus acris* Meadow Buttercup**
Rare. St Agnes, St Martin's and St Mary's.

***Ranunculus bulbosus* Bulbous Buttercup**
Locally frequent. Recorded from all the inhabited islands. Plants attributable to the variety *dunensis* have occasionally been found on coastal sites.

***Ranunculus arvensis* Corn buttercup**
Extinct.

***Ranunculus parviflorus* Small-flowered buttercup**
Locally frequent. Found on all the inhabited islands, but rare St Agnes.

***Ranunculus sceleratus* Celery-leaved buttercup**
Rare. Two casual records from St Agnes may have been introduced by birds.

***Ranunculus sardous* Hairy buttercup**
Rare/locally frequent. Scattered records from the inhabited islands, but more frequent on St Agnes. Occurs in two types of habitat; wet grassland and bulbfields

Ranunculus muricatus **Prickly-fruited or Scilly buttercup**
Locally frequent. Only widespread on St Mary's, apparently declining in arable fields on the other inhabited islands.

Ranunculus marginatus var *trachycarpus* **St Martin's buttercup**
Rare. Only known from arable fields on a farm on St Martin's.

Ranunculus ficaria **Celandine**
Frequent. Widespread on all the inhabited islands; also found on Samson and Annet. Most plants are subspecies(ssp) *ficaria* without tubers in the leaf axils, but ssp *ficariiformis* occurs on St Mary's.

Ranunculus flammula **Lesser spearwort**
Locally frequent. Occurs in wetland sites on all inhabited islands. A very small form found around Abbey Pool has not yet been specifically determined.

Ranunculus hederaceus **Ivy-leaved crowfoot**
Rare. Only known from a few wet sites on St Mary's, declining.

Ranunculus tripartitus **Thread-leaved water-crowfoot**
Extinct.

Ranunculus baudotii **Seaside buttercup**
Rare. Formerly widespread in pools on all the inhabited islands. Now only regularly recorded from Pool Green on St Martin's and Little Pool, Bryher.

Ranunculus trichophyllus **Fennel-leaved water crowfoot**
Extinct.

Thalictrum minus **Lesser meadow-rue**
Extinct.

PAPAVERACEAE

Papaver somniferum **Opium Poppy**
Occasional. Scattered records from St Mary's, Tresco, St Martin's and St Agnes.

Papaver rhoeas **Common Poppy**
Locally frequent. On all the inhabited islands on arable and disturbed land.
Plants on St Martin's and St Mary's sometimes have large black spots at the
base of the petals.

Papaver dubium **Long-headed poppy**
Locally frequent. This is the common poppy of the arable fields. Apparently
absent from Tresco.

Glaucium flavum **Yellow-horned poppy**
Occasional/locally frequent. There is a fluctuating population on sandy
beaches on the inhabited islands, as well as Teän and Great Ganilly.

FUMARIACEAE

This interesting and difficult genus is well-represented in Scilly. For a
guide to identification refer to Murphy 2009

Fumaria capreolata ssp *babingtonii* **White ramping-fumitory**
Locally frequent. Most common St Agnes and St Mary's, but found on all the
inhabited islands. Can be confused with *F. occidentalis*. Has been recorded in
past from Puffin Island off Samson, and Great Ganinick.

Fumaria occidentalis **Western ramping fumitory**
Locally frequent. The main population is on St Mary's. Has occurred on St
Martin's in two places recently but may not have persisted.

Fumaria bastardii **Tall ramping-fumitory**
Locally abundant. Widespread on the inhabited islands, but less frequent on
Tresco and Bryher. Two varieties, *bastardii* and *hibernica* have been
recorded.

Fumaria muralis boraei **Common ramping-fumitory**
Locally abundant. Probably the most widespread and most variable fumitory
in Scilly found on all the inhabited islands. The variety *major* has been
recorded occasionally.

Fumaria officinalis **Common fumitory**
Rare/locally frequent. Only reliably known from Bryher where both subspecies *officinalis* and *wirtgenii* have been recorded. There is one recent record from St Agnes.

Fumaria purpurea **Purple fumitory**
Extinct? Formerly recorded from fields at Old Town, St Mary's but not seen there since 1988. Other records appear to have been misidentifications of *F.muralis boraei*.

ULMACEAE

Ulmus spp. **Elm**
The elm populations in Scilly are currently being investigated. The main species on St Mary's seem to be *Ulmus* x *hollandica* Dutch Elm. Elms are found on all the inhabited islands where they have been planted and have spread, often by suckering. Other elms such as *U. procera* English Elm and *U. glabra* Wych Elm have also been recorded but need confirmation. *Ulmus minor* has been recorded from St Mary's and St Martin's, with subspecies *augustifolia* and *sarniensis* having been identified on St Mary's.

CANNABACEAE

Humulus lupulus **Hop**
Occasional. Garden escape on Tresco and St Mary's.

MORACEAE

Ficus carica **Fig**
Rare. Where recorded away from gardens on Tresco and St Martin's is probably birdsown.

URTICACEAE

Urtica dioica **Common nettle**
Locally abundant. Widespread on all the inhabited islands, Teän, St Helen's, Samson and Annet as well as some small islets, although there are no recent records from the Eastern Isles.

***Urtica urens* Small nettle**
Locally frequent. Found on all the inhabited islands. No recent records from uninhabited islands.

***Parietaria judaica* Pellitory-of-the-wall**
Locally frequent. Found on walls on most of the inhabited islands, but apparently missing from St Agnes.

***Parietaria officinalis* Eastern pellitory-of-the-wall**
Rare. A plant found near Abbey Garden's, Tresco in 2007 is presumed a recent accidental introduction.

***Soleirolia soleirolii* Mind-your-own-business**
Occasional. Garden escape now established on the inhabited islands but apparently absent from Bryher.

FAGACEAE

***Fagus sylvatica* Beech**
Planted Tresco and St Mary's.

***Quercus cerris* Turkey oak**
Planted Tresco and on St Agnes.

***Quercus ilex* Evergreen oak**
Planted Tresco.

***Quercus petraea* Sessile oak**
Planted St Mary's.

***Quercus robur* Pedunculate oak**
Planted St Mary's and Tresco. A stunted tree that has been known on Great Gannick for many years has not been seen recently.

BETULACEAE

Betula sp. **Silver/Downy birch**
Planted St Mary's.

Alnus glutinosa **Alder**
Rare. Wetland, St Mary's and Tresco. Also planted St Mary's.

Alnus incana **Grey alder**
Planted Tresco.

Corylus avellana **Hazel**
Planted St Mary's.

NYCTAGINACEAE

Mirabilis jalapa **Miracle-of-Peru**
Occasional. Garden escape St Mary's.

AIZOACEAE
Many species of 'mesems' or succulents are grown on walls and in gardens around the inhabited islands. It is not always clear which plants are planted and which have become naturalised, as even small pieces of plant are easily propagated. Several species of succulents have been found on uninhabited islands where they are taken by gulls. Most apparently do not persist, possibly due to exposure to salt spray in winter.

Aptenia cordifolia **Heart-leaf ice-plant**
Established as garden escape on all the inhabited islands.

Ruschia caroli **Shrubby dewplant**
Established garden escape on Tresco and St Mary's.

Lampranthus falciformis **Sickle-leaved dewplant**
Established on St Mary's, St Martin's and Tresco. Many colourful garden cultivars are grown and may be found as garden escapes.

Lampranthus roseus **Rosy dewplant**
Established on St Mary's. One record from St Helen's.

Oscularia deltoides **Deltoid-leaved dewplant**
Established on the inhabited islands.

Disphyma crassifolium **Purple dewplant**
Established on Tresco, Bryher and St Mary's. It has also been recorded from Round Island.

Drosanthemum floribundum **Pale dewplant**
Established on St Mary's, St Martin's and Tresco. It has also been recorded on St Helen's and Great Ganinick.

Erepsia heteropetala **Lesser sea-fig**
Established at only one quarry site on St Mary's.

Carpobrotus acinaciformis **Sally-my-handsome**
Recorded on all the inhabited islands, much less common than *C. edulis*.

Carpobrotus edulis **Hottentot fig**
Established on all the inhabited and several uninhabited islands including St Helen's, Teän, some Eastern Isles and occasionally other islands. Occurs in different colour forms and varieties including var *edulis,* var *rubescens* and var *chrysophthalmus*.

Carpobrotus glaucescens **Angular sea-fig**
Apparently this species naturalised in a few places on Tresco.

Tetragonia tetragonioides **New Zealand spinach**
Rare. Occasional records from Tresco and Teän.

CHENOPODIACEAE

Chenopodium quinoa **Quinoa**
Currently only known as a planted crop as a conservation mixture/bird food on St Mary's.

***Chenopodiun bonus-henricus* Good King Henry**
Extinct? Single 1960s record from Tresco.

***Chenopodium rubrum* Red goosefoot**
Local. Found on the inhabited and some of the larger uninhabited islands including Samson, Great Arthur, Great Ganilly and Teän.

***Chenopodium polyspermum* Many-seeded goosefoot**
Rare. Tresco and St Mary's, also a record from Great Ganilly.

***Chenopodium hybridum* Maple-leaved goosefoot**
Rare. Only recorded once from Tresco and recently on Bryher.

***Chenopodium murale* Nettle-leaved goosefoot**
Occasional. Recorded from cultivated ground on all the inhabited islands.

***Chenopodium album* Fat-hen**
Locally frequent. Found on all the inhabited islands and occasionally on smaller, uninhabited islands where gulls nest.

***Atriplex prostrata* Spear-leaved orache**
Locally abundant. Widely recorded from all inhabited and most uninhabited islands.

***Atriplex x gustafssoniana* (*A.prostrata x A. longipes*)**
Rare. A record from Teän 2008 needs confirmation.

***Atriplex glabriuscula* Babington's orache**
Occasional. Probably under- recorded, found on shores on both inhabited and some uninhabited islands.

***Atriplex laciniata* Frosted orache**
Locally frequent. A strandline species on both inhabited and uninhabited islands.

***Atriplex halimus* Shrubby orache**
Rare. Garden escape or planted on a site on St Mary's.

Beta vulgaris ssp *maritima* Sea beet
Abundant. Widespread around the shore on all the inhabited and uninhabited islands including some of the small, rocky islets. Occasionally found inland. Used locally as 'spinach'.

Beta vulgaris ssp *vulgaris* Root beet
Occasional escape from cultivation St Mary's and Tresco.

Suaeda maritima Annual sea-blite
Rare. Only one record, Shipman Head, Bryher 1984. Probably bird sown.

Salsola kali ssp *kali* Prickly saltwort
Rare. Recent records from sandy beaches on Tresco, St Martin's, Teän, Samson and Great Ganilly. Has disappeared from many of its former sites especially on the inhabited islands.

AMARANTHACEAE

Amaranthus retroflexus Common amaranth
Rare. Birdseed alien St Mary's and Tresco.

Amaranthus hybridus Green amaranth
Rare. Tresco.

Amaranthus caudatus Love-lies-bleeding
Garden escape St Agnes.

Amaranthus albus White pigweed
Rare. Birdseed alien St Mary's.

PORTULACACEAE

Portulacea oleracea Common purslane
Rare. Fields on Tresco, St Mary's and St Agnes.

Claytonia perfoliata Spring beauty
Locally frequent. All inhabited islands on arable land.

Claytonia sibirica Pink purslane
Rare. Recorded from St Mary's and St Agnes.

Montia fontana Blinks
Locally frequent. Recorded from the inhabited islands and also Samson. The subspecies generally recorded on Scilly is ssp *amporitana* although ssp *variabilis* and *chondrosperma* have been recorded.

CARYOPHYLLACEAE

Arenaria serpyllifolia Thyme-leaved sandwort
Rare. Known only from a few discrete sandy areas on Bryher, St Martin's, St Agnes and St Mary's. No recent records from former localities on Samson or Teän.

Honckenya peploides Sea sandwort
Locally frequent. Found on beaches on all inhabited and several uninhabited islands.

Stellaria media Common chickweed
Locally frequent. Found on all the inhabited islands and some uninhabited islands including Annet and some of the smaller Eastern Isles (around gull nests).

Stellaria neglecta Greater chickweed
Rare. Only recently recorded from St Mary's.

Stellaria pallida Lesser chickweed
Rare. Recorded from all the inhabited islands and from Teän.

Stellaria holostea Greater stitchwort
Rare. Only one record from St Mary's where it was probably introduced with planted trees.

Stellaria uliginosa Bog stichwort
Rare. Only known from wetland sites on Higher and Lower Moors and Holy Vale, St Mary's.

Cerastium tomentosum **Snow–in-summer**
Rare. Garden escape St Agnes and St Mary's.

Cerastium fontanum **Common mouse-ear**
Locally frequent. Found on the inhabited and occasionally uninhabited islands. The subspecies *holosteoides* and *vulgare* have been recorded.

Cerastium glomeratum **Sticky mouse-ear**
Abundant. All inhabited islands.

Cerastium diffusum **Sea mouse-ear**
Locally frequent. Recorded from all the inhabited and some larger uninhabited islands.

Cerastium semidecandrum **Little mouse-ear**
Rare. Only a few records from Bryher, St Mary's, St Martin's and St Agnes. This may be partly due to the plant flowering very early and being missed by most visiting botanists.

Sagina procumbens **Procumbent pearlwort**
Frequent. Found on all the inhabited islands and larger uninhabited islands.

Sagina apetala **Annual pearlwort**
Frequent. Occurs on all the inhabited islands. Subspecies *apetala* and *erecta* have both been recorded in Scilly.

Sagina maritima **Sea pearlwort**
Frequent. Found on the inhabited islands, usually coastal, but occasionally inland. It has also been recorded on Annet.

Polycarpon tetraphyllum **Four-leaved allseed**
Abundant. Occurs on all the inhabited islands on disturbed ground, arable fields and even in pavement cracks and has also been recorded on Teän and Northwethel.

Spergula arvensis **Corn spurrey**
Frequent/locally abundant. Found on all the inhabited islands mainly in arable fields.

Spergularia rupicola **Rock sea-spurrey**
Frequent. Found on all the inhabited and most of the uninhabited islands including the Norrads and Western Rocks.

Spergularia marina **lesser sea-spurrey**
Rare. Only known from along the leat and fringes of the brackish pool on Bryher.

Spergularia rubra **Sand spurrey**
Local. Found on paths and compacted ground around arable fields on the inhabited islands.

Spergularia bocconei **Greek sea-spurrey**
Rare. Only known from compacted and bare ground near the coast on St Mary's.

Lychnis flos-cuculi **Ragged Robin**
Rare. Now apparently only found on Lower Moors, St Mary's (formerly recorded from Higher Moors as well).

Agrostemma githago **Corncockle**
Extinct. A record from St Mary's in 1988 almost certainly had been accidentally introduced with garden material or seeds.

Silene uniflora **Sea campion**
Locally frequent. Mostly coastal, but occasionally grows on walls or rocks inland. Recorded from all the inhabited and many uninhabited islands including Annet.

Silene latifolia ssp *alba* **White campion**
Rare. Only recorded from a few localities on St Agnes, St Mary's, St Martin's and Tresco. Frequently recorded in error due to confusion with the much more common white-flowered form of *Silene dioica*.

Silene dioica **Red Campion**
Abundant. Found on all inhabited and larger uninhabited islands including Annet. Occurs in many shades from white, through pink to red.

Silene coeli-rosa **Rose-of-heaven**
Rare garden escape St Mary's 1973.

Silene gallica **Small-flowered or English catchfly**
Locally frequent. Found mainly as arable weed on all the inhabited islands.
Several colour varieties have been recognised: var *gallica* pale pink, var
anglica off-white and var *quinquevulnera* which has a crimson spot on each
petal. This latter variety is now extinct in the wild but occasionally escapes
from gardens on St Mary's where it has been conserved.

Saponaria officinalis **Soapwort**
Extinct. Formerly on Tresco but there are no recent records.

Dianthus plumarius **Pink**
Garden escape, St Mary's 1997.

Dianthus barbatus **Sweet-William**
Garden escape, Holy Vale and Porth Mellon, St Mary's in 1990s.

POLYGONACEAE

Persicaria amphibia **Amphibious bistort**
Very rare. Established by Abbey Pool, Tresco.

Persicaria maculosa **Redshank**
Locally frequent. Although recorded from all the inhabited islands is only
widespread on St Mary's. There is a 1992 record from Northwethel.

Persicaria lapathifolia **Pale persicaria**
Occasional. Only known from Tresco and St Mary's.

Persicaria hydropiper **water-pepper**
Local. Wet places St Mary's and Tresco. Also recorded from a beach on
Samson.

Polygonum maritimum **Sea knotgrass**
Rare. Two recent records; from sandy beaches on Bryher 2003 and St
Martin's 2007.

Polygonum oxyspermum **Ray's knotgrass**
Rare. Only recent record was from a sandy beach on Tresco in 2004.

Polygonum arenastrum **Equal-leaved knotgrass**
Frequent. Apparently less common than *P. aviculare* but probably overlooked.
Recorded from the inhabited islands, also from Northwethel.

Polygonum aviculare **Knotgrass**
Abundant. Found on all the inhabited islands, also recorded on Northwethel
with *P.arenastrum* (needs investigating further).

Fallopia japonica **Japanese knotweed**
The plant has been subject to an extermination programme by the IOS Council
and is no longer common. It appeared to have gone from St Agnes before the
herbicide programme. A few patches persist in places on St Mary's.

Fallopia baldschuanica **Russian vine**
Garden escape. Bryher and St Mary's.

Fallopia convolvulus **Black bindweed**
Occasional. Appears to be now much less common than formerly with only
scattered records from the inhabited islands. Apparently absent from Tresco.
Has also been recorded from Northwethel.

Fagopyrum esculentum Buckweed
Extinct. Recorded in 1952 near a chicken run on St Mary's.

Muehlenbeckia complexia **Wireplant**
Locally abundant. Covers large areas of hedges and hillsides on Tresco and St
Mary's, but has apparently gone from St Agnes.

Rumex acetosella **Sheep's sorrel**
Locally abundant. Found on all the inhabited and most of the larger
uninhabited islands.

Rumex acetosa Common sorrel
Abundant. All inhabited and most uninhabited islands, only absent from the rocky uninhabited islands. The ssp *hibernicus* has been identified at Rushy Bay, Bryher and may occur at other dune sites.

Rumex frutescens Argentine dock
Rare. Only known from Gugh.

Rumex hydrolapathum Water dock
Extinct? Old records from St Mary's.

Rumex crispus Curled dock
Abundant. Widespread in cultivated and coastal habitats. Inland plants are ssp *crispus*, but on the coast ssp *littoreus* is the common plant. In the past ssp *littoreus* was frequently misrecorded as *R.rupestris*.

Rumex conglomeratus Clustered dock
Occasional. Recorded from inhabited islands but not St Martin's.

Rumex sanguineus Wood dock
Rare. Only recorded recently from wooded area on Tresco.

Rumex rupestris Shore dock
Rare. Only known from Samson, Teän and Annet. A small colony on Tresco is dwindling and the population is generally in decline.

Rumex pulcher Fiddle dock
Locally frequent. Common on the inhabited islands where the fiddle-shaped leaves are easily recognised in spring. Formerly known from Teän.

Rumex obtusifolius Broad-leaved dock
Frequent. Found on all the inhabited islands.

Rumex crispus x *rupestris*
Rare. This hybrid has been recorded a few times from St Agnes and Samson.

Rumex x *muretii*
Rare. Only recorded once from St Mary's.

Rumex* x *ogulinensis
Extinct? Recorded by Lousley from St Martin's in 1936.

Rumex* x *pratensis
Rare. Recorded from two sites on St Mary's in 1995.

***Rumex* x *pseudopulche*r**
Rare. One record from Tresco by Lousley in 1939.

***Rumex* x **trimenii**
Rare. Only one relatively recent record from Tresco in 1984. There are
Lousley records from Samson and Tresco in 1936.

PLUMBAGINACEAE

***Armeria maritima* Thrift**
Locally dominant. Found on coastal sites all around the inhabited islands and
on most uninhabited islands. Also grows inland on a few places such as wall-
tops on St Mary's.

ELATINACEAE

***Elatine hexandra* Six-stamened waterwort**
Rare. Last recorded in 1990 from Abbey Pool, Tresco. It may still be present.

CLUSIACEAE

***Hypericum androsaemum* Tutsan**
Garden escape recorded from two places on St Mary's.

***Hypericum* x *inodorum* Tall Tutsan**
Garden escape recorded from several places on St Mary's and near the
Gardens on Tresco.

***Hypericum hircinum* Stinking Tutsan**
Garden escape recorded from several places on St Mary's in the 1990s.

Hypericum perforatum *Perforate St John's-wort*
Rare. One plant found in the restored area at east of Porthcressa in 2000 is believed to have been an accidental introduction.

Hypericum humifusum **Trailing St John's-wort**
Locally frequent. Recorded from all the inhabited islands from both heathland, arable fields and man-made habitats such as between kerb stones.

Hypericum pulchrum **Slender St John's-wort**
Rare. Apparently restricted to the east of the islands. Only known from coastal heathland on St Mary's, St Martin's and the Eastern Isles.

MALVACEAE

Malva moschata **Musk Mallow**
Rare. Recorded only from St Mary's and St Martin's.

Malva sylvestris **Common Mallow**
Locally frequent. Known from all the inhabited islands.

Malva pusilla **Small Mallow**
Extinct. Last recorded from St Martin's in 1939.

Malva neglecta **Dwarf Mallow**
Frequent. On all the inhabited islands.

Lavatera arborea **Tree mallow**
Locally frequent. Recorded from mainly coastal habitats on inhabited and larger uninhabited islands. Often a feature on small rocky islands in the Norrad and Western Rocks where few other plants can survive.

Lavatera cretica **Smaller Tree-mallow or Cretan Mallow**
Locally frequent. Found on all the inhabited islands.

Hibiscus trionum **Bladder Ketmia or Flower of the Hour**
Alien. A casual record from Tresco in 1984.

VIOLACEAE

Viola odorata **Sweet violet**
Occasional. A garden escape now established on St Mary's, St Martin's and St Agnes.

[*Viola hirta* **Hairy violet** recorded in error for *V. odorata*.]

Viola riviniana **Common dog-violet**
Frequent. The common violet on all inhabited and most uninhabited islands.

Viola reichenbachiana **Early dog-violet**
Rare. Plants identified as this species in Scilly are being reviewed.

Viola canina **Heath dog-violet**
Plants identified as this species in Scilly are also being reviewed.

Viola tricolor **Wild pansy**
Rare. Possible confused with bicoloured *V. arvensis?* Not recorded recently.

Viola x wittrockiana **Garden pansy**
Rare garden escape St Mary's.

Viola arvensis **Field pansy**
Occasional/locally frequent. Occurs as an arable weed on Tresco, St Martin's and St Mary's. Apparently absent from Bryher and St Agnes.

Viola kitaibeliana **Dwarf pansy**
Rare. The only substantial population is on Bryher around Rushy Bay (seriously depleted by storm damage in 2008, but hopefully will recover). Small populations also exist on Tresco and Teän. A former site on St Martin's has not been relocated.

TAMARICACEAE

Tamarix gallica **Tamarisk**
Frequent. Still found in hedges on all the inhabited islands, but far less than previously, having being replaced by evergreen hedging plants. There are

occasional apparently naturalised plants. A tree on Samson by the ruined houses was presumably planted there by the former inhabitants.

Tamarix africana **African tamarisk**
Rare. One identified in a hedgerow near the sea at Old Grimsby, Tresco in 1992/3 may still be there.

SALICACEAE

Populus alba **White poplar**
Rare. Planted along Pool Road and near Great Pool, Tresco.

Populus x canescens **Grey poplar**
Rare. Planted near Great Pool, Tresco.

Populus x canadensis **Hybrid black poplar**
Rare. Planted Tresco and St Mary's. Includes variety '*Serotina*' on Tresco.

Populus x jackii **'Balm of Gilead'**
Rare. Planted on Toll's Island, St Mary's.

Populus balsamifera **Eastern balsam poplar.**
One planted on a farm on St Mary's.

Salix fragilis **Crack willow**
Occasional. Apparently introduced to St Mary's, St Martin's and Tresco.

Salix x rubens
Rare. Planted St Mary's.

Salix x rubens basfordiana
Rare. Planted St Mary's.

Salix alba **White willow**
Rare. Known from St Mary's where introduced.

Salix triandra **Almond willow**
Rare. One introduction to St Mary's.

Salix viminalis Osier
Rare. Introduced to St Agnes, St Mary's and St Martin's for basketwork and willow-weaving.

Salix x smithiana
Rare. Planted Tresco and St Mary's.

Salix caprea Goat willow
Not recorded. Some planted hybrids may have been mistaken for this species.

Salix cinerea ssp oleifolia Rusty willow
Locally frequent. The common willow on Scilly. Probably native in wetland sites on St Mary's, Tresco and Bryher. Also a few individuals on St Helen's and Great Ganilly.

Salix x multinervis
Rare. Apparently this hybrid is planted on Lower Moors.

Salix x reichardtii
Rare. Apparently this hybrid is also on Lower Moors.

BRASSICACEAE

Sisymbrium officinale Hedge mustard
Frequent. On all the inhabited islands.

Arabidopsis thaliana Thale cress
Locally frequent. Recorded from all the inhabited islands; very easily missed and may be more common than the records suggest.

Erysimum cheiranthoides Treacle mustard
Rare. Only recorded on farmland on St Mary's (two places) and from a farm on Bryher.

Erysimum cheiri Wallflower
Garden escape, Tresco and St Mary's. May be established on the Garrison.

Matthiola incana Hoary stock
Garden escape, established on St Mary's, St Agnes, and also recorded from Tresco and Bryher.

Matthiola longipetala Night-scented stock
Rare garden escape on St Mary's.

Barbarea vulgaris Wintercress
Rare. Known only from near the church on Tresco and from Trenoweth, St Mary's.

Barbarea verna American wintercress
Rare. No recent records from former sites and only recently recorded at Dolphin Town, Tresco and near Juliet's Garden, St Mary's.

Rorippa nasturtium-aquaticum Water-cress
Local. Possibly reduced since Lousley's time, many of the roadside gutters are no longer suitable for wetland plants since the roads were asphalted. Still present in wetland sites on St Mary's and Tresco. Some of the plants on St Mary's are exceptionally large and robust.

Rorhippa sylvestris Creeping yellow-cress
Rare. Only known as an arable weed at Trenoweth.

Armoracia rusticana Horse-radish
Rare garden escape. School Green, Tresco and near Porthloo, St Mary's.

Cardamine pratense Lady's smock/Cuckooflower
Local. Wet sites Tresco and St Mary's.

Cardamine flexuosa Wavy bittercress
Occasional. St Mary's, Tresco and St Agnes.

Cardamine hirsuta Hairy bittercress
Frequent. More common than *C. flexuosa* although found in similar places, especially in cultivated fields. On all the inhabited islands.

Lunaria annua **Honesty**
Rare garden escape. Bryher, St Martin's and St Mary's.

Lobularia maritima **Sweet Alyssum**
Locally frequent. A common plant especially round Hugh Town, also found on St Martin's and Bryher

Cochlearia officinalis **Common scurvygrass**
Locally abundant. Mainly coastal sites on the inhabited islands and uninhabited islands, especially the smaller Eastern Isles, Norrads and Western Rocks. In 1989 ssp *scotica* was recorded from Toll's Island.

Cochlearia danica **Danish scurvygrass**
Locally abundant. All the inhabited islands and larger uninhabited islands including man-made habitats such as in pavement cracks and wall bases in Hugh Town.

Capsella bursa-pastoris **Shepherd's purse**
Frequent. Still a very common arable weed on all the inhabited islands.

Thlaspi arvense **Field penny-cress**
Occasional/locally frequent. Arable fields on the inhabited islands. Appears to be less common than formerly, except on St Mary's where it is locally frequent.

Iberis umbellata **Garden candytuft**
Garden escape Old Town, St Mary's.

Lepidium heterophyllum **Smith's pepperwort**
Rare, Only now found on the Garrison.

Coronopus squamatus **Swine-cress**
Frequent. Recorded on all the inhabited islands, but apparently rare on St Martin's.

Coronopus didymus **Lesser swine-cress**
Abundant. Found on the inhabited islands, more so than *C. squamatus,* although both species may be found growing together in places.

***Diplotaxis tenuifolia* Perennial wall-rocket**
Extinct.

***Diplotaxis muralis* Annual wall-rocket or Stinkweed**
Local. Found mainly in vicinity of buildings at New Grimsby, Tresco, on St Martin's and several places on St Mary's including in Hugh Town.

***Brassica napus* ssp *oleifera* Oil-seed Rape**
Only one record from Porthloo in 1997, presumed an accidental introduction.

***Brassica rapa* Turnip**
Rare. Escape from cultivation St Mary's and St Martin's.

***Brassica rapa* ssp *oleifera* Turnip rape**
Rare. One record from Hugh Town, St Mary's.

***Brassica nigra* Black mustard**
Occasional. Records from St Mary's, Bryher and Tresco.

***Sinapsis arvensis* Charlock**
Occasional. Occurs locally as an arable weed on all the inhabited islands but possibly less common than formerly.

***Sinapsis alba* White mustard**
Rare. Only recorded from fields near Great Pool, Tresco in 1995.

***Cakile maritima* Sea rocket**
Locally frequent/occasional. Found on sandy shores on the inhabited islands, also Teän, Great Ganilly and Little Arthur. Populations fluctuate in numbers and locality from year to year as is usual in strandline species.

***Crambe maritima* Sea kale**
Occasional. Found on sandy/shingle beaches on all the inhabited islands and Great Ganilly. Numbers fluctuate from year to year.

***Raphanus raphanistrum* ssp *raphanistrum* Radish**
Locally frequent. St Agnes, St Helen's and St Mary's. The varieties *flavus* and *raphanistrum* have been recorded.

***Raphanus raphanistrum* ssp *maritimum* Sea radish**
Locally frequent. Occurs on St Agnes, St Mary's, St Martin's and Teän. May be confused with ssp *raphanistrum,* from which it can be distinguished when the fruits are ripe.

***Raphanus sativus* Radish**
Rare. St Mary's, presumed escape from cultivation.

RESEDACEAE

***Reseda alba* White mignonette**
Rare. St Mary's.

***Reseda lutea* Wild mignonette**
Rare. Only known from Gugh.

CLETHRACEAE

***Clethra arborea* Lily-of-the-valley-tree**
Garden escape on Tresco, especially Tresco Wood.

ERICACEAE

***Rhododendron ponticum* Rhododendron**
Locally dominant. Plantations on Abbey Wood and Monument Hill, Tresco. Also occurs elsewhere on Tresco, also St Mary's and Bryher.

***Gaultheria shallon* Shallon**
Garden escape. Tresco.

***Calluna vulgaris* Heather or Ling**
Locally dominant. One of the main heathland species on all the inhabited and larger uninhabited islands.

***Erica cinerea* Bell heather**
Locally dominant. One of the main heathland plants on all the inhabited islands and larger uninhabited islands including Round Island.

Erica arborea **Tree heather**
Garden escape. Established in woodland area outside Abbey Gardens.

Erica vagans **Cornish Heath**
Garden escape. Tresco.

MYRSINACEAE

Myrsine africana
Relict of cultivation. Tresco.

PRIMULACEAE

Primula vulgaris **Primrose**
Local. Old Town churchyard, St Mary's, Appletree Banks, Tresco and Samson. Almost certainly of garden origin.

Lysimachia nemorum **Yellow pimpernel**
Rare. Presumed garden escape from Abbey Gardens in 1984.

Lysimachia nummularia **Creeping-Jenny**
Rare. Tresco and St Mary's.

Lysimachia vulgaris **Yellow loosestrife**
Rare. In wetland at Lower Moors, St Mary's.

Anagallis tenella **Bog pimpernel**
Occasional. On damp ground on Tresco, St Agnes and St Mary's.

Anagallis arvensis **Scarlet pimpernel**
Abundant. Recorded from all the inhabited islands and also from Samson, St Helen's, Nornour and Great Ganilly. The colour forms *azurea* (deep blue) and *carnea* (flesh pink) are found occasionally.

Anagallis minima **Chaffweed**
Rare. Only recorded recently from damp tracks on St Agnes and St Martin's, formerly also near Abbey Pool, Tresco.

Glaux maritima Sea-milkweed
Locally frequent. Scattered places around the coast on the inhabited islands and also Northwethel, Great Ganilly and Teän. Also found around the edges of pools on Tresco, Bryher and St Agnes.

Samolus valerandi Brookweed
Occasional. Occurs on at a few wet sites on Tresco, St Mary's and St Agnes and also around freshwater seepages on Annet and Menawethan.

PITTOSPORACEAE

Pittosporum crassifolium Karo/Pittosporum
Frequent. Found both as a planted hedge and as naturalised plants on the inhabited and larger uninhabited islands. Is commonly bird-sown on remote places including on rocky carns.

Pittosporum tenuifolium
Rare escape from cultivation.

HYDRANGEACEAE

Hydrangea macrophylla Hydrangea
Rare garden escape.

GROSSULARIACEAE

Escallonia macrantha
Planted mainly as hedging on the inhabited islands, occasional escapes from cultivations are recorded.

CRASSULACEAE

Crassula decumbens Scilly pigmyweed
Rare. Alien introduction only known from tracks near Halangy Down Ancient Village and Bant's Carn Farm. Gradually spreading along pathway towards the golf course.

Umbilicus rupestris **Navelwort /Wall pennywort**
Abundant. Grows on walls and rocks on all inhabited and larger uninhabited islands. Occasionally grows on ground on heathland.

Aeonium cuneatum **Aeonium**
Garden escape. Naturalised plants can be difficult to distinguish from planted specimens. Also a number of additional *Aeonium* species and cultivars have been introduced to Scilly as garden plants. As pieces of the plant soon become rooted it spreads vegetatively very easily. Occasionally recorded from uninhabited islands where it has been taken by gulls.

Aeonium arboretum **Tree aeonium**
Garden escape. As with the previous species identifying genuinely naturalised plants is difficult. Found on all the inhabited islands and has been recorded on Ragged Island, where it was presumed to have been taken by gulls.

Sedum confusum **Lesser Mexican stonecrop**
Garden escape. Recorded from Old Town, St Mary's 1996.

Sedum acre **Biting stonecrop**
Occasional. Much less common than *S. anglicum* although both occasionally grown together. Recently recorded from Bryher, Tresco and St Mary's, also from Samson, Teän and Great Ganilly.

Sedum album **White stonecrop**
Rare. Recent records from St Mary's, and from St Agnes.

Sedum anglicum **English stonecrop**
Abundant. All inhabited and most uninhabited islands including from some of the smaller rocky islets such as in the Norrad rocks.

SAXIFRAGACEAE

Bergenia crassifolia **Elephant ear**
Garden escape Tresco.

ROSACEAE

Spiraea salicifolia Bridewort
Garden escape, St Mary's.

Spiraea x pseudosalicifolia Confused bridewort
Garden escape, St Mary's.

Spiraea douglasii Steeple-bush
Garden escape, St Mary's.

Filipendula ulmaria Meadowsweet
Rare. Only known from Holy Vale, St Mary's.

Rubus fruticosus agg Blackberry
Abundant. Found on all inhabited and the larger uninhabited islands. Locally dominant in some places. A number of 'splits' have been identified.

Rumus ulmifolius Elm-leaved bramble.
Frequent. The most often recorded bramble especially on the Eastern Isles.

Potentilla anserina Silverweed
Locally frequent. Wet grassland on all the inhabited islands, also Northwethel, Samson and Great Ganilly. A form with both sides of the leaf silver occurs in places.

Potentilla erecta Tormentil
Locally frequent. A typical heathland species on the inhabited islands and larger uninhabited islands other than Annet.

Potentilla anglica Trailing tormentil
Rare? No recent records.

Potentilla reptans Creeping cinquefoil
Locally frequent. Only common in south of St Mary's. Otherwise only recently recorded from St Agnes, Tresco and Bryher.

Aphanes arvensis **Parsley-piert**
Occasional. All inhabited islands, in similar places to the next species.

Aphanes australis **Slender parsley-piert**
Locally frequent. Found in arable field and disturbed ground on all the inhabited islands.

Rosa multiflora **Many-flowered rose**
Rare garden escape. Established in a hedge on St Mary's.

Rosa rugosa **Japanese rose**
Garden escape Tresco and St Mary's.

Rosa canina **Dog rose**
Occasional. On the inhabited islands including Gugh, apparently absent from Bryher. May still be present on St Helen's.

Rosa rubiginosa **Sweet briar**
Garden escape. Bryher.

Prunus spinosa **blackthorn**
Rare. Probable planted or an escape from cultivation, St Mary's, St Martin's and Tresco.

Prunus domestica **Wild plum**
Rare. One, possibly ssp *insititia* on the Garrison.

Malus sylvestris **Crab apple**
Rare. St Martin's and St Mary's.

Malus domestica **Apple**
Occasional. All inhabited islands except St Agnes.

Sorbus aucuparia **Rowan**
Planted tree on St Mary's.

Cotoneaster simonsii **Himalayan cotoneaster**
Garden escape Tresco.

Cotoneaster horizontalis **Wall cotoneaster**
Garden escape Tresco and St Mary's.

Crataegus monogyna **Hawthorn**
Occasional. Found as a hedge or solitary tree mainly on St Mary's and St Martin's.

MIMOSACEA

Albizia lophantha
Garden escape. Tresco.

Acacia melanoxylon **Australian blackwood**
Garden escape. Tresco.

FABACEAE

Lotus corniculatus **Common bird's-foot clover**
Abundant. Found on all the inhabited and larger uninhabited islands in several habitats including heathland, coast and grasslands.

Lotus pedunculatus **Greater bird's-foot clover**
Locally abundant. All inhabited and some larger uninhabited islands. Often in drier habitats as well as the usual wetland places.

Lotus subbiflorus Hairy bird's-foot clover
Frequent. All inhabited islands and Teän. Found in arable fields as well as heathland and coastal habitats.

Ornithopus perpusillus **Bird's-foot**
Locally frequent. All inhabited islands, Teän and Samson in sandy or heathy areas.

Ornithopus pinnatus **Orange bird's-foot**
Locally frequent. St Agnes, St Martin's, Tresco, Bryher, Teän, Samson and Great Ganilly. Apparently absent from St Mary's. Found in sandy and heathy areas, often with *O. perpusillus*. Populations fluctuate from year to year.

Vicia cracca **Tufted vetch**
Occasional. On all the inhabited islands (other than St Agnes) and Teän.

Vicia hirsuta **Hairy tare**
Locally frequent. All inhabited islands in grassy and arable places.

Vicia tetrasperma **Smooth tare**
Occasional. Found on the inhabited islands other than Tresco. Also recorded from St Helen's.

Vicia sepium **Bush vetch**
Occasional. Recorded from all the inhabited islands. Has been confused with *V. sativa* at times.

Vicia sativa **Common vetch**
Abundant. Two subspecies occur. Ssp *nigra* is found on all the inhabited and some larger uninhabited islands. Ssp *segetalis* has only been recorded from the inhabited islands. Although Ssp *sativa* has been recorded in the past these are now believed to be errors for *segetalis*.

Vicia lathyroides **Spring sedge**
Rare. Only recorded from one site on Bryher and two on Tresco.

Vicia bithynica **Bithynian vetch**
Rare. Last recorded from a field on St Martin's 2001.

Vicia faba **Broad bean**
Occasional escape from cultivation.

Lathyrus japonicus **ssp *maritimus* Sea pea**
Rare. The plants that were discovered on St Mary's in 2007 and 2008 were the first time the plant had been seen since 1985. There was also an unconfirmed 2007 record from St Martin's.

Lathyrus pratensis **Meadow vetchling**
Rare. Only known from a few grassy areas on St Mary's.

Lathyrus latifolius **Broad-leaved everlasting pea**
Rare. One record from Bryher.

Lathyrus annuus **Fodder pea**
Rare. Casual. No recent records.

Pisum sativum var arvense **Field pea**
Rare. One record from St Mary's in 1982.

Ononis repens **Common restharrow**
Rare. Only known from St. Martin's, St Mary's (Maypole area) and Samson.

Melilotus officinalis **Ribbed melilot**
Formerly occurred on Gugh, but now apparently only known as an
introduction with 'conservation' seed-mixes.

Medicago lupulina **Black medick**
Occasional. Found on the inhabited islands with the apparent exception of
Bryher.

Medicago sativa sativa **Lucerne**
Rare. Last recorded from St Agnes in 1990.

Medicago polymorpha **Toothed medick**
Locally frequent. All inhabited islands.

Medicago arabica **Spotted medick**
Locally abundant. All inhabited islands. Sometimes the black spots on the
leaf are very large.

Trifolium ornithopodoides **Bird's-foot clover/ Birdsfoot fenugreek**
Locally frequent. Found on all the inhabited islands, formerly recorded on
Teän.

Trifoium repens **White clover**
Locally dominant. Found on all the inhabited and larger uninhabited islands.
Cultivated forms have been sown in fields on the inhabited islands. The
variety *townsendii* with red or purple flowers and even purple leaves is very
common in coastal habitats.

Trifolium occidentale Western clover
Frequent. Found mostly on coastal grassland around the inhabited islands, also on Teän, Samson and the Arthurs in the Eastern Isles. Flowers very early in the year, usually before *T. repens.*

Trifolium hybridum Alsike clover
Rare. There are a few records from the inhabited islands other than Tresco, possibly as a relic from cultivation.

Trifolium glomeratum Clustered clover
Rare. A few scattered records from St Mary's, St Martin's and Tresco.

Trifolium suffocatum Suffocated clover
Occasional. Found on all the inhabited islands usually in sandy places but probably overlooked.

Trifolium fragiferum Strawberry clover
Extinct.

Trifolium campestre Hop trefoil
Locally frequent. Scattered records from all the inhabited islands and Teän .

Trifolium dubium Lesser trefoil
Locally abundant. Found on all the inhabited islands. Recorded from Samson.

Trifolium micranthum Slender trefoil
Occasional. Scattered localities on the inhabited islands, also recorded on Nornour.

Trifolium pratense Red clover
Locally frequent. All inhabited islands, some plants appear to be the cultivated form var *sativa,* and red clover is often included in seed mixtures.

Trifolium medium Zigzag clover
Rare. There are a few recent records from inhabited islands with exception of St Martin's. May have been previously overlooked.

Trifolium incarnatum Crimson clover
Rare. Occurred on St Martin's in 2008, an accidental introduction.

Trifolium striatum **Knotted clover**
Occasional. Scattered records from inhabited islands except Bryher.

Trifolium scabrum **Rough clover**
Occasional. Scattered records from Bryher, St Martin's and St Mary's.

Trifolium arvense **Hare's-foot clover**
Locally frequent. All the inhabited islands except Bryher.

Trifolium subterraneum Subterraneum clover
Locally frequent. On grassland on all inhabited islands and Samson.

Lupinus arboreus **Tree lupin**
Occasional. Established on all inhabited islands.

Cytiscus scoparius **Broom**
Locally frequent. Only common on St Mary's and Bryher, has recently been found on Samson.

Spartium junceum **Spanish broom**
Garden escape. One record St Mary's.

Ulex europaeus **Gorse**
Locally dominant. Heathland areas on all the inhabited and larger uninhabited islands.

Ulex gallii **Western gorse**
Locally frequent. Restricted to coastal heathland mainly on St Mary's, with more scattered records from the other inhabited islands, also from St Helen's, Northwethel and Little Arthur.

ELAEAGNACEAE

Hippophae rhamnoides **Sea buckthorn**
Planted. Tresco outside the Gardens on the edge of dunes.

Elaeagnus pungens
There are no records of this shrub outside gardens.

GUNNERACEAE

Gunnera tinctoria Giant rubarb
Alien. Occasional garden escape, usually from material dumped from gardens.

LYTHRACEAE

Lythrum salicaria Purple loosestrife
Local. Wetland sites Tresco and St Mary's.

Lythrum hyssopifolium Grass-poly
Rare. Recorded as casual from an arable field on St Martin's in 1984, a record for St Mary's in 2008 could not be confirmed.

Lythrum portula Water-purslane
Rare. Only known from wet areas around the Abbey Pool and nearby Hill, Tresco and on Wingletang, St Agnes.

MYRTACEAE

Leptospermum scoparium Broom tea-tree
Rare. Established escape from cultivation Abbey Hill area, Tresco.

Leptospermum lanigerum Woolly tea-tree
Rare. Established escape from cultivation Abbey Hill area, Tresco.

Eucalyptus globulus Southern blue-gum
Rare. Abbey Hill and woodland area, Tresco.

Eucalyptus viminalis Ribbon gum
Rare. Abbey Hill and woodland area, Tresco.

Eucalyptus pulchella White peppermint gum
Rare. Abbey Hill area, Tresco also St Martin's.

Eucalyptus spp.
Other species of Eucalyptus are planted on Tresco and may become established. *E. viminalis* and *E. urnigera* have been recorded.

Luma apiculata **Chilean myrtle**
Locally occasional. Established escape from cultivation on Tresco, St Martin's and St Mary's. In some places is spreading.

ONAGRACEAE

Epilobium hirsutum **Great willowherb or Codlins and cream**
Occasional. Scattered records from St Mary's, Tresco and Bryher.

Epilobium parviflorum **Hoary willowherb**
Rare. A few records from St Mary's and Tresco.

Epilobium montanum **Broad-leaved willowherb**
Occasional. A scatter of records from St Mary's, St Agnes and Tresco.

Epilobium lanceolatum **Spear-leaved willowherb**
Rare. Only known from St Mary's and St Agnes.

Epilobium tetragonum **Square-stalked willowherb**
Locally frequent. Found on all the inhabited islands, ssp *lamyi* has been recorded.

Epilobium obscurum **Short-leaved willowherb**
Occasional. Records from the inhabited islands other than Bryher.

Epilobium ciliatum **American willowherb**
Occasional. Tresco, St Mary's and St Agnes.

Epilobium palustre **Marsh willowherb**
Rare. Formerly known from Higher and Lower Moors, the only recent record was from Lower Moors, St Mary's in 2007.

Chamerion angustifolium **Rosebay willowherb**
Rare. One casual record from the Garrison, St Mary's.

Oenothera **species. Evening- primrose**
Due to the difficulty in separating the species and hybrids only recent or confirmed records are identified to species. Frequently escapes from gardens.

Oenothera glazoviana **Large-flowered evening- primrose**
Occasional. Recorded from all the inhabited islands except Bryher.

Oenothera biennis **Common evening-primrose**
Rare. Recorded from Tresco.

Oenothera cambrica **Small-flowered evening-primrose**
Rare. One site on St Mary's.

Oenothera x cambrica
Rare. This hybrid has been identified from a site on St Mary's.

Oenothera x fallax **Intermediate evening- primrose**
Rare. One record from St Mary's.

Fuchsia magellanica **Fuchsia**
Planted as hedge species on the inhabited islands, occasionally may have naturalised.

Circaea lutetiana **Enchanter's nightshade**
Rare. Only recorded from The Garrison, St Mary's where it appears to be spreading as garden weed.

CORNACEAE

Griselelinia littoralis **New Zealand broadleaf**
Rare. Naturalised or planted Tresco Wood.

CELASTRACEAE

Euonymus japonicus **Japanese spindle**
Planted as hedge species on the inhabited islands.

AQUIFOLIACEAE

Ilex aquifolium **Holly**
Rare. Garden escape occasionally birdsown on Tresco, St Mary's and St Martin's, also occurs on Samson and formerly on Great Ganilly.

BUXACEAE

***Buxus sempervirens* Box**
Garden escape. Tresco and St Mary's.

EUPHORBIACEAE

***Mercuralis annua* Annual mercury**
Locally abundant/ occasional. Found in arable fields and disturbed ground on southern half of St Mary's, with scattered records from the other inhabited islands. One record from Samson.

***Euphorbia mellifera* Honey spurge**
Garden escape Tresco.

***Euphorbia helioscopa* Sun spurge**
Locally frequent. Recorded mainly from cultivated ground on all the inhabited islands.

***Euphorbia lathyris* Caper spurge**
Garden escape. St Mary's and St Martin's.

***Euphorbia peplus* Petty spurge**
Locally frequent. Recorded from all inhabited islands, especially from Tresco and St Mary's.

***Euphorbia portlandica* Portland spurge**
Locally abundant. Mainly coastal sites on all the inhabited and larger uninhabited islands. Found inland in Hugh Town.

***Euphorbia paralias* Sea spurge**
Locally frequent. Coastal sites on all inhabited and larger uninhabited islands.

***Euphorbia cyparissias* Cypress spurge**
Garden escape. St Mary's.

Euphorbia amygdaloides **Wood spurge**
Occasional. A local species of dunes and heathland on Bryher, Tresco, St
Helen's, St Martin's, Great Ganinick and Great Ganilly.

LINACEAE

Linum catharticum **Purging flax**
Rare. Only known from Great Bay area, St Martin's.

Radiola linoides **Allseed**
Locally frequent. Damp and sandy places on all the inhabited islands, Toll's
Island, St Mary's, St Helen's and Great Ganilly

POLYGALACEAE

Polygala vulgaris **Common milkwort**
Locally frequent. Found mainly on heathland on all the inhabited islands and
some larger uninhabited islands.

Polygala serpyllifolia **Heath milkwort**
Occasional. Recent records only from St Mary's, St Martin's and
Northwethel. Confusion between the two species of milkwort may lead to
under-recording of this species.

HIPPOCASTANACEAE

Aesculus hippocastanum **Horse chestnut**
Planted tree. Tresco.

ACERACEAE

Acer campestre **Field maple**
Planted tree. St Mary's.

Acer pseudoplatanus **Sycamore**
Planted tree and garden escape. Tresco, St Mary's and St Martin's.

ANACARDIACEAE

Rhus typhina Stag's horn sumach
Garden escape St Mary's.

RUTACEAE

Correa backhouseana **Tasmanian-fuchsia**
Occasional. Frequently hedging or ornamental shrub. Naturalised in woodland on Tresco and on the Garrison, St Mary's.

OXALIDACEAE

Oxalis rosea **Annual pink-sorrel**
Garden escape, Tresco.

Oxalis corniculata **Procumbent yellow-sorrel**
Occasional. Garden escape established on Tresco and St Mary's. The purple-leaved sub-species *atropurpurea* occurs in several places on St Mary's.

Oxalis exilis **Least yellow-sorrel**
Occasional. Garden escape established in several places on Tresco.

Oxalis megalorrhiza **Fleshy yellow-sorrel**
Frequent. Established on walls on Tresco, St Mary's, St Martin's and St Agnes. Often planted but also appears to be spreading naturally.

Oxalis articulate **Pink-sorrel**
Frequent. Escape from cultivation now established on all the inhabited islands.

Oxalis debilis **Large-flowered pink-sorrel**
Rare. Garden escape found on St Agnes, Tresco and St Mary's.

Oxalis latifolia Garden pink-sorrel
Locally occasional. Garden escape established on a few places on St Mary's, St Agnes and Tresco. There is some confusion between this and the other pink oxalis found in Scilly.

Oxalis tetraphylla Four-leaved pink-sorrel
Rare. Garden escape only recorded from vicinity of Abbey Gardens, Tresco.

Oxalis pes-caprea Bermuda buttercup
Locally abundant. Now well-established as arable weed and on disturbed ground on all the inhabited islands.

GERANIACEAE

Geranium rotundifolium Round-leaved cranesbill
Rare. One casual record from St Martin's.

Geranium molle Dove's-foot cranesbill
Locally frequent. Found on the inhabited islands and on Teän, St Helen's and Great Ganilly.

Geranium dissectum Cut-leaved cranesbill
Locally frequent. Found on all the inhabited islands.

Geranium lucidum Shining cranesbill
Garden escape on the Garrison, Hugh Town.

Geranium robertianum Herb-Robert
Rare. Scattered records from St Mary's.

Geranium rubescens Greater herb-Robert
Garden escape. Tresco, Bryher and St Mary's.

Geranium maderense Giant herb-Robert
Locally frequent. Garden escape now established and spreading on the inhabited islands.

Erodium maritimum Sea storksbill
Locally frequent. Found on all the inhabited islands, Teän and Great Ganilly. Often found on man-made habitats such as pavement cracks.

Erodium moschata Musk storksbill
Locally frequent. On all the inhabited islands in arable fields and disturbed ground.

Erodium cicutarium Common storksbill
Locally frequent. On all the inhabited islands, also Teän, Samson and Great Ganilly. The subsp *dunense* has been recorded occasionally.

Erodium lebeli Sticky storksbill
Rare. A few records from Gugh, St Martin's and St Mary's.

Pelargonium tomentosum Peppermint-scented geranium
Garden escape naturalised in woodland on Tresco.

TROPAEOLACEAE

Tropaeolum majus Nasturtium
Garden escape on the inhabited islands.

ARALIACEAE

Hedera helix Ivy
Abundant. All inhabited islands, Eastern Isles, Teän, St Helen's and Northwethel.
ssp *helix* has been recorded from St Mary's, but the common ivy in Scilly is ssp *hibernica*.

Fatsia japonica
Garden escape. St Mary's and Tresco.

APIACEAE

Hydrocotyle vulgaris Marsh pennywort
Locally frequent. Damp places on heathland and wetlands on all the inhabited islands.

Eryngium maritimum Sea holly
Locally frequent. Coastal sites on all the inhabited islands other than St Mary's. There is also a casual record from the Garrison, presumably from garden material.

Anthriscus sylvestris Cow parsley
Occasional. Scattered records from St Martin's, St Agnes and the northern part of St Mary's.

Anthriscus caucalis Bur Chervil
Occasional. Mainly found on St Martin's with a few records from Tresco and St Agnes. Recently recorded from Teän.

Scandix pecten-veneris Shepherd's needle
Rare. Other than a few casual records from St Mary's is only found in a few arable fields on St Martin's.

Smyrnium olusatrum Alexanders
Frequent. Found on all the inhabited islands and Samson.

Conopodium majus Pignut
Rare. Only now found on heathland and grassland on St Martin's.

Aegopodium podagraria Ground elder
Rare. Scattered records from Tresco, St Mary's and St Agnes. May be confused with vegetative Alexanders.

Berula erecta Lesser water-parsnip
Rare. Wetland areas St Mary's and Tresco. There has been some confusion between this species and *Apium nodiflorum.*

Crithmum maritimum Rock samphire
Locally abundant. Coastal sites around the inhabited and all larger uninhabited islands.

Oenanthe fistula Tubular water-dropwort
Rare. Wetland areas Tresco and St Mary's.

Oenanthe lachenalii Parsley water-dropwort
Extinct.

Oenanthe crocata Hemlock water-dropwort
Locally frequent. Wetland, including damp fields on the inhabited islands, but apparently absent from Tresco.

Foeniculum vulgare Fennel
Locally frequent. Found on all the inhabited islands, especially common on St Mary's.

Conium maculatum Hemlock
Rare. Occurs on St Mary's, St Helen's and Samson.

Bupleurum subovatum False thorow-wax.
Casual, probably extinct.

Apium graveolens Wild celery
Rare. One record from the Garrison in 1994 without confirmation.

Apium nodiflorum Fool's water-cress
Local. Found in wet areas and along watercourses on Tresco and St Mary's. May sometimes be misidentified as *Berula*.

Apium inundatum Lesser marshwort
Rare. Only found in wetland areas on Bryher, Tresco and St Mary's.

Petroselinum crispus Garden parsley
Garden escape. Persists on the Garrison, St Mary's and on St Martin's.

Ammi majus Bullwort
Casual. One casual record from St Mary's 1987.

Angelica sylvestris Wild angelica
Locally frequent/occasional. Scattered sites on St Martin's, Tresco and St Mary's. Also recorded on Great Ganinick.

Pastinaca sativa Wild parsnip
Rare. A few records from St Mary's.

Heracleum sphondylium Hogweed
Abundant. Found on all inhabited and larger uninhabited islands.

Torilis nodosa Knotted hedge-parsley
Rare. Has only been recorded from St Agnes and St Martin's.

Torilis japonica Upright hedge-parsley
Rare. One recent record from St Mary's.

Pimpernella saxifraga Burnet saxifrage.
Extinct. Last record was of three plants in 1956 between Porth Mellin and Thomas' Porth, St Mary's.

Daucus carota Wild carrot
Abundant. Found on all the inhabited islands and Samson. Apparently absent from the other uninhabited islands. Although ssp *carota* is most frequently recorded especially inland, coastal plants are usually ssp *gummifera.*

GENTIANACEAE

Centaurium erythraea Common centaury
Abundant. All inhabited and larger uninhabited islands. Very variable in size, with stunted plants in exposed sites.

APOCYNACEAE

Vinca minor Lesser periwinkle
Garden escape. St Mary's.

Vinca major Greater periwinkle.
Garden escape. Found on all the inhabited islands. The var *oxyloba* has been recorded on St Mary's.

SOLANACEAE

Nicandra physalodes Shoo-fly plant
Occasional. Occurs on St Mary's and Tresco.

Physalis peruviana **Cape-gooseberry**
Rare. Recorded as casual St Mary's.

Lycopersicon esculentum **Tomato**
Garden escape that is frequently found on beaches, St Mary's, Tresco and Samson.

Solanum nigrum **Black nightshade**
Locally frequent. On all the inhabited islands and recently recorded on Samson.

Solanum physalifolium **Green nightshade**
Occasional. Recorded from St Mary's, Tresco and St Martin's.

Solanum sarachoides **Leafy-fruited nightshade**
Rare. Formerly an arable weed St Martin's, but not recorded recently.

Solanum laciniatum **Kangaroo berry**
Occasional. Found as a garden escape on Tresco and St Mary's.

Solanum dulcamara **Bittersweet**
Locally frequent. Found on all inhabited and all the larger uninhabited islands. The var *marinum* occurs commonly on shingle and rocky beaches.

Solanum tuberosa **Potato**
Garden escape. Found on rubbish dumps, beaches and waste land, St Mary's and St Martin's.

Datura stramonium **Thorn apple**
Rare. Recorded from Tresco, St Mary's and Teän and formerly St Agnes.

CONVOLVULACEAE

Convolvulus arvensis **Field bindweed**
Locally frequent. Found on all the inhabited islands.

Calystegia soldanella **Sea bindweed**
Locally frequent. Restricted to dunes and coastal sites on the inhabited islands and some uninhabited islands.

Calystegia sepium **Hedge bindweed**
Locally frequent. Found on all the inhabited islands. Two subspecies occur, ssp *sepium* has been recorded from all the inhabited islands (including one record of the form *colorata*) and ssp *roseata* that is found on St Mary's (probably the commonest subspecies there) and also St Agnes, St Martin's and Bryher, but is apparently absent from Tresco.

Calysegia silvatica **Large bindweed**
Occasional. Recorded from all the inhabited islands.

CUSCUTACEAE

Cuscuta epithymum **Dodder**
Rare. Now only know as a parasite on gorse on one area of St Martin's.

BORAGINACEAE

Echium vulgare **Viper's bugloss**
Rare. Only known from Gugh and a field on St Agnes.

Echium plantagineum **Purple viper's bugloss**
Extinct? Formerly recorded as an arable weed on Tresco, St Martin's and St Mary's but now apparently gone. Recent records appear to be of garden origin.

Echium pininana **Giant viper's bugloss**
Garden escape. This and other garden species occasionally occur as seedlings on the inhabited islands, but tend not to persist.

Symphytum officinale **Common comfrey**
Error, - probably for the next.

Symphytum x *uplandicum* **Russian comfrey**
Garden escape. St Mary's and Tresco.

Anchusa arvensis **Bugloss**
Locally frequent. All inhabited islands.

Pentaglottis sempervirens **Green alkanet**
Rare. Established Appletree Banks, Tresco.

Borage officinalis **Borage**
Occasional. Found as garden escape on all the inhabited islands, most commonly St Mary's. There is also a record from Ragged Island in the Eastern Isles.

Myosotis scorpioides **Water-forget-me-not**
Rare. Only recorded from Tresco.

Myosotis secunda **Creeping forget-me-not**
Rare. Tresco and St Mary's.

Myosotis arvense **Field forget-me-not**
Occasional. Found on the inhabited islands other than St Martin's and also from Teän. There are former records from St Martin's and most of the uninhabited islands.

Myosotis ramosissima **Early forget-me-not**
Locally frequent. Found on all the inhabited islands, Great Ganilly and Teän, but not recorded recently from St Mary's.

Myosotis discolor **Changing forget-me-not**
Locally frequent. All the inhabited islands and St Helen's, Teän, Great Ganilly and Annet.

Myosotis laxa **Tufted forget-me-not**
Rare. Recently recorded from Shooter's Pool, St Mary's.

VERBENACEAE

Verbena officinalis **Vervain**
Rare. Only recorded from a few places on St Mary's.

LAMIACEAE

Stachys arvensis **Field woundwort**
Locally frequent. Arable fields and disturbed ground on all the inhabited islands.

Stachys officinalis **Betony**
Rare. Only known from Great Ganilly, Eastern Isles and a former site on Chapel Down, St Martin's. A recent record from St Mary's needs confirmation.

Stachys palustris **Marsh woundwort**
Rare. Recent records only from Tresco and St Mary's.

Stachys sylvatica **Hedge woundwort**
Rare. Recent records only from St Martin's and St Mary's.

Ballota nigra meridionalis **Black horehound**
Rare. Only recorded from St Mary's and St Martin's.

Lamiastrum galeobdolon argentatum **Yellow archangel**
Garden escape. St Mary's.

Lamium album **White dead-nettle**
Extinct.

Lamium purpureum **Red dead-nettle**
Occasional. Recorded from all inhabited islands.

Lamium hybridum **Cut-leaved dead-nettle**
Occasional. Recorded from all inhabited islands.

Lamium amplexicaule **Henbit dead-nettle**
Rare. Bryher and St Martin's.

Scutellaria galericulata **Skullcap**
Rare. Wet areas on shore and around Southward Well, Samson and Abbey Pool area, Tresco.

Teucrium scorodonia **Wood sage**
Locally frequent. On all inhabited islands and larger uninhabited islands including Annet.

Ajuga reptans **Bugle**
Garden escape. A cultivar with coloured leaves has been recorded on St Mary's.

Glecoma hederacea **Ground-ivy**
Locally frequent. All inhabited and larger inhabited islands.

Prunella vulgaris **Selfheal**
Locally frequent. All inhabited islands, Samson and Great Ganilly.

Melissa officinalis **Balm**
Extinct garden escape.

Clinopodium ascendens **Common calamint**
Rare. St Mary's and St Agnes.

Thymus polytrichus **Wild thyme**
Rare. Only in any amount on Gugh; also found on Great Ganilly and on Peninnis, St Mary's.

Thymus x *citriodorus* **Lemon thyme**
Garden escape. St Mary's.

Lycopus europaeus **Gypsywort**
Occasional. Wet areas on Tresco, St Mary's and two sites on St Martin's.

Mentha aquatica **Water mint**
Rare. Wetland sites St Mary's and St Martin's.

Mentha x *suavis*
Rare. One record of this hybrid has been recorded near Old Town, St Mary's.

Mentha x *piperita* **Peppermint**
Rare. Garden escape St Mary's.

Mentha spicata **Spear mint**
Occasional. Garden escape found on the inhabited islands except Bryher.

Mentha x *villosa* **Apple mint**
Occasional. Found on St Agnes, St Mary's and St Martin's. The variety *alopecuroides* has been recorded from St Mary's and St Martin's.

Mentha x *rotundifolia* **False apple-mint**
Rare. Garden escape St Agnes and St Mary's.

Mentha suaveolens **Round-leaved mint**
Rare. St Mary's, Tresco and St Martin's.

Mentha pulegium **Pennyroyal**
Extinct.

Mentha requienii **Corsican mint**
Rare. Garrison, St Mary's. Last recorded in 2002 (area was sprayed with weedkiller).

Rosmarinus officinalis **Rosemary**
Garden escape. Occasional records from St Mary's and St Martin's.

Salvia reflexa **Mintweed**
Rare. One record from birdseed, St Mary's.

Salvia verbenaca **Wild Clary**
Extinct.

CALLITRICHACEAE

There has been some confusion over identification of water starworts in Scilly. There is also some fluctuation in species composition of the different water bodies. Only recently confirmed species are listed here. All other records are included under *Callitriche* agg.

Callitriche stagnalis **Common water-starwort**
Occasional. Recorded from Tresco, St Mary's and Samson.

Callitriche platycarpa **Various-leaved water starwort**
Rare. Recorded from Bryher in 1977.

Callitriche obtusangula **Blunt-fruited water-starwort**
Rare. Occurs in several places on St Mary's.

Callitriche brutia **Pedunculate water-starwort**
Rare. Recorded from Great Pool, Tresco and Higher Moors, St Mary's.

Callitriche hamulata **Intermediate water-starwort**
Occasional. Recorded from Tresco, Little Pool on Bryher, Higher Moors and Watermill stream, St Mary's.

PLANTAGINACEAE

Plantago coronopus **Buck's-horn plantain**
Abundant. All inhabited and most uninhabited islands. Can occur as very tiny plants sometimes without the characteristic lobed leaves.

Plantago maritima **Sea plantain**
Rare. Apparently restricted to a few coastal sites on St Mary's, mainly on the east coast. There is a record from Tresco that needs confirmation.

Plantago major **Greater plantain**
Abundant. On all inhabited islands, plus Samson, Northwethel and Teän. The subspecies *major* and *intermedia* have been recorded.

Plantago lanceolata **Ribwort plantain**
Abundant. On all inhabited and many uninhabited islands, including Samson, Teän, Northwethel and the Arthurs.

Littorella uniflora **Shoreweed**
Rare. Only recorded from Abbey Pool.

BUDDLEJACEAE

Buddleja davidii **Buddleja**
Garden escape. St Mary's and Tresco.

Buddleja globosa **Orange-ball tree**
Garden escape. St Mary's.

OLEACEAE

Jasminum officinale **Summer jasmine**
Garden escape. St Mary's.

Fraxinus excelsior **Ash**
Rare. Planted in a few places on St Mary's and Tresco.

Ligustrum vulgare **Wild privet**
Locally frequent. Restricted to sites on Tresco, St Martin's and St Mary's,
also Teän and St Helen's. Formerly recorded on Samson.

Ligustrum ovalifolium **Garden privet**
Planted shrub. Occasional garden escape St Mary's and St Martin's.

SCROPHULARIACEAE

Verbascum blattaria **Moth mullein**
Rare casual. Tresco

Verbascum virgatum **Twiggy mullein**
Rare casual. Tresco. No recent records.

Verbascum phlomoides **Orange mullein**
Rare casual. St Mary's.

Verbascum thapsus **Great mullein**
Occasional. Found on all the inhabited islands, also St Helen's and Teän.

Scrophularia nodosa **Common figwort.**
Apparently extinct. Formerly St Mary's and Tresco.

61

Scrophularia auriculata **Water figwort**
Rare. Possibly a recent arrival. Found at two places on St Mary's.

Scrophularia scorodonia **Balm-leaved figwort**
Locally abundant. Found on all the inhabited islands and larger uninhabited islands.

Limosella aquatica **Mudwort**
Rare.   Only known from Abbey Pool, Tresco, but no recent records.

Mimulus guttatus **Monkeyflower**
Probably extinct. Formerly recorded on Lower Moors, St Mary's.

Misopates orontium **Weasel's-snout**
Occasional. Records from all the inhabited islands. Occasionally appears in abundance from buried seed.

Cymbalaria muralis **Ivy-leaved toadflax**
Occasional. Found only on Tresco, St Mary's and St Martin's. The white form *flore alba* is found on St Mary's and St Martin's.

Kickxia elatine **Sharp-leaved fluellen**
Occasional. Found on the inhabited islands but apparently absent from St Martin's.

Kickxia spuria **Round-leaved fluellen**
Rare. Only recent record is from St Agnes.

Linaria vulgaris **Common toadflax**
Rare. St Mary's and St Agnes.

Digitalis purpurea **Foxglove**
Abundant. Found on all the inhabited and most uninhabited islands

Veronica serpyllifolia **Thyme-leaved speedwell**
Occasional. Found on the inhabited islands, also Samson. Scilly plants are ssp *serpyllifolia.*

Veronica officinalis **Heath speedwell**
Locally occasional. Only known from a few discrete areas on Tresco, St Mary's and Gugh.

Veronica chamaedrys **Germander speedwell**
Locally frequent. All inhabited islands, Samson, St Helen's and Great Ganilly.

Veronica montana **Wood speedwell**
Rare. Abbey Wood, Tresco.

Veronica beccabunga **Brooklime**
Casual. Introduced, Longstone Centre, St Mary's.

Veronica arvensis **Wall speedwell**
Locally frequent. All inhabited islands, also Teän.

Veronica agrestis **Green field speedwell**
Occasional. All inhabited islands.

Veronica polita **Grey field speedwell**
Rare. Tresco, St Agnes, and St Mary's.

Veronica persica **Common field speedwell**
Occasional. All inhabited islands.

Veronica hederifolia **Ivy-leaved speedwell**
Rare. All inhabited islands.

Hebe x lewisii **Lewis's Hebe**
Planted as hedging. Occasional escape from cultivation.

Hebe x franciscana **Hedge veronica**
Planted as hedging. May occasionally escape from cultivation.

Sibthorpia europaea **Cornish moneywort**
Rare. Now only found on one site on St Mary's.

Euphrasia officinalis agg Eyebright
This difficult group is widespread on all the inhabited and larger uninhabited islands. Some earlier identifications are now not accepted and efforts are being made to get specialist confirmation of voucher specimens.

Recent identifications have included:

Euphrasia tetraquetra Eyebright
Occasional. Recorded from the inhabited islands, some records have been confirmed.

Euphrasia nemorosa x confusa Eyebright
Recorded from St Agnes & St Mary's.

Odontites vernus Red Bartsia
Rare. Recorded from a wall top on St Mary's in 2007 without confirmation.

Parentucellia viscosa Yellow bartsia
Locally frequent. Bryher, Tresco and St Mary's.

Pedicularis sylvatica Lousewort
Locally frequent. All inhabited islands and also Samson.

OROBANCHACEAE

Orobanche minor Lesser broomrape
Rare. The only recent records are from Tresco, St Mary's, Bryher and possibly Gugh..

Orobanche hederae Ivy broomrape
Probably extinct.

ACANTHACEAE

Acanthus mollis. Bear's breech
Garden escape. Established on St Mary's, Tresco, St Martin's and St Agnes. Many of the clumps are long-established,

CAMPANULACEAE

***Campanula rapunculoides* Rampion bellflower**
Garden escape. Garrison, St Mary's.

***Campanula poscharskyana* Trailing bellflower**
Garden escape. St Agnes and St Mary's.

***Wahlenbergia hederacea* Ivy-leaved bellflower**
Probably extinct.

***Jasione montana* Sheep's-bit**
Locally frequent. Only found on St Mary's and west St Martin's.

RUBIACEAE

***Coprosma repens* Tree bedstraw**
Planted shrub. Planted as hedge on the inhabited islands, often birdsown away from cultivation including on the uninhabited islands.

***Sherardia arvensis* Field madder**
Occasional. Found on all the inhabited islands.

***Galium palustre* Marsh bedstraw**
Occasional. Only found in wetlands on Tresco and St Mary's. Both ssp *palustre* and ssp *elongatum* have been recorded.

***Galium verum* Lady's bedstraw**
Locally frequent. All the inhabited islands other than St Agnes. Also Gugh, Samson and Teän.

***Galium mollugo* Hedge bedstraw**
Rare. Recorded as casual from St Mary's and St Martin's.

***Galium saxatile* Heath bedstraw**
Occasional. Inhabited islands other than St Agnes, Gugh and Samson.

Galium aparine **Goosegrass/Cleavers**
Locally frequent. All inhabited islands and most well-vegetated uninhabited islands.

Rubia peregrina **Wild madder**
Locally frequent. Coastal on inhabited and most uninhabited islands.

CAPRIFOLIACEAE

Sambucus nigra **Elder**
Occasional. All inhabited islands, Samson and St Helen's.

Viburnum tinus **Laurustinus**
Garden escape. St Agnes.

Lonicera periclymenum **Honeysuckle**
Abundant. All inhabited and most uninhabited islands.

Lonicera caprifolium **Perfoliate honeysuckle**
Garden escape. Tresco.

Valerianella locusta **Common cornsalad**
Rare. Mainly arable fields on all inhabited islands. The variety *dunensis* was formerly recorded from Teän.

Valerianella carinata **Keel-fruited cornsalad**
Rare? Formerly recorded from St Agnes and St Mary's.

Valerianella dentata **Tooth-fruited cornsalad**
Extinct? No recent records.

Valeriana officinalis **Common valerian**
Rare. As a casual Old Town, St Mary's.

Valeriana dioica **Marsh valerian**
Rare. Single occurrence on cleared area Lower Moors, probably from buried seed.

Centranthes ruber Red valerian
Locally frequent. All the inhabited islands, especially near habitations and in a quarry.

DIPSACACEAE

Dipsacus fullonum Teasel
Rare. Recent records only from Bryher and St Mary's.

ASTERACEAE

Osteospermum ecklonis Cape daisy
Garden escape. Established in places on the inhabited islands. There are several different cultivars but the one generally known as 'Tresco Purple' is frequent.

Actium minus Lesser burdock
Locally frequent. All inhabited islands and Samson.

Actium nemorosa Wood burdock
Rare. Plants recorded as this species St Mary's and Tresco.

Carduus tenuifolius Slender or Seaside thistle
Rare. Recorded from the inhabited islands except St Agnes. Also from Teän and Great Ganilly.

Cirsium vulgare Spear thistle
Locally abundant. All the inhabited islands and larger uninhabited islands including the Eastern Isles.

Cirsium palustre Marsh thistle
Rare. Higher Moors to Holy Vale, St Mary's.

Cirsium arvense Creeping thistle
Locally frequent. All inhabited islands, Teän and the Eastern Isles. The var mite without prickles was known from St Martin's but appears to have died out.

***Centaurea cyanus* Cornflower**
Extinct.

***Centaurea nigra* Common knapweed**
Occasional. Recorded from scattered localities on all the inhabited islands including Gugh.

***Cichorium intypus* Chicory**
Rare. Only known as casual from St Mary's and St Martin's.

***Lapsana communis* Nipplewort**
Rare. St Mary's, Tresco and St Agnes.

***Hypochaeris radicata* Cat's-ear**
Abundant. All inhabited and most larger uninhabited islands, except Annet.

***Leontodon autumnalis* Autumn hawkbit**
Occasional. Inhabited islands other than St Martin's, plus Samson, Teän and Northwethel. Probably under-recorded.

***Leontodon hispidus* Rough hawkbit**
Rare. Recent records only from Gugh and Bryher.

***Leontodon saxatilis* Lesser hawkbit**
Locally frequent. All the inhabited islands and larger uninhabited islands other than Annet.

***Picris echioides* Bristly oxtongue**
Locally frequent. Bryher, St Martin's, St Mary's and Gugh, plus Samson

***Sonchus arvensis* Perennial sow-thistle**
Occasional. Recorded from all the inhabited islands and St Helen's.

***Sonchus oleraceas* Prickly sow-thistle**
Abundant. Found on all inhabited and most uninhabited islands including Round island.

Sonchus asper **Smooth sow-thistle**
Locally frequent. All the inhabited and most uninhabited islands.

Taraxacum officinale agg. **Dandelion**
Locally frequent. All the inhabited islands and also Teän and Samson.
This difficult group needs investigation in Scilly as there are clearly a number
of different dandelions present.

Crepis biennis **Rough hawk's-beard**
Rare. One casual record of this species from a roadside ditch on St Mary's

Crepis capillaris **Smooth hawk's-beard**
Locally abundant. All the inhabited islands, Samson, Teän and Great Ganilly.

Crepis vesicaria **Beaked hawk's-beard**
Occasional/ locally frequent. Only on the inhabited islands.

Pilosella officinarum **Mouse-ear hawkweed**
Rare. Only recorded recently from dune grassland near the Plains, St Martin's
and a field near Bant's Carn, St Mary's..

Hieracium umbellatum **spp** ***bichlorophyllum*** **Hawkweed**
Local. Only known from heathy areas on St Mary's.

Gazania rigens **Treasureflower/Gazania**
Garden escape. Established in a few areas on the inhabited islands. Also
recorded from Round Island. Most places it is the yellow variety with a black
spot on the petal, the plain yellow var *uniflora* also occurs.

Filago vulgaris **Common cudweed**
Locally frequent. A common plant on St Mary's but only scattered records
from St Agnes, Tresco and Bryher.

Gnaphalium sylvaticum **Heath cudweed**
Extinct. Only known as casual from two sites on St Mary's but apparently did
not persist.

Gnaphalium uliginosum **Marsh cudweed**
Rare/ Locally abundant. Common on St Mary's but rare or occasional on the other inhabited islands.

Gnaphalium luteoalbum **Jersey cudweed**
Rare. A recent arrival to one site on St Mary's.

Helichrysum bracteatum **Everlasting flower**
Garden escape. Recorded from St Martin's.

Helichrysum petiolare **Silver-bush everlastingflower**
Garden escape. Several places on Tresco and St Mary's, has also been recorded from St Helen's and Samson.

Inula helenium **Elecampane**
Extinct.

Pulicaria dysenterica **Common Fleabane**
Rare. Great Pool, Tresco, Shooter's Pool and Lower Moors, St Mary's.

Solidago virgaurea **Goldenrod**
Locally frequent. Heathland and coastal sites St Mary's, St Martin's and Eastern Isles

Solidago canadensis **Canadian goldenrod**
Garden escape. St Mary's.

Aster x *versicolor* **Late Michaelmas daisy**
Rare. Garden escape St Mary's and St Martin's.

Aster novi-belgii **Confused Michaelmas daisy**
Rare. Established garden escape St Agnes.

Aster lanceolatus **Narrow-leaved Michaelmas daisy**
Rare. Garden escape St Agnes.

Chrysocoma coma-aurea **Shrub goldilocks**
Garden escape, Tresco and St Mary's.

***Erigeron glaucus* Seaside daisy**
Garden escape. St Martin's and St Mary's.

***Erigeron karvinskianus* Mexican fleabane**
Garden escape. Tresco, St Martin's and St Mary's.

***Conyza canadensis* Canadian fleabane**
Rare. St Mary's and Tresco.

***Conyza bonariensis* Argentine fleabane**
Rare. Scattered localities on St Mary's, apparently spreading.

***Conyza sumatrensis* Guernsey fleabane**
Rare. A recent arrival in Scilly that is now spreading on Tresco and Bryher.

***Olearia paniculata* Akiraho**
Rare. Garden escapeTresco.

***Olearia* x *haastii* Daisy bush**
Rare. Garden escape or planted? Tresco and St Mary's.

***Olearia macrodonta* New Zealand holly**
Rare. Garden escape or planted Tresco and St Mary's.

***Olearia traversii* Ake-ake**
Locally frequent. Garden origin or planted as hedging on the inhabited islands.

***Olearia solandri* Coastal daisy bush**
Rare. One site St Mary's, probably planted.

***Bellis perennis* Daisy**
Abundant. All inhabited islands and most larger uninhabited islands (not Annet).

***Tanacetum parthenium* Feverfew**
Garden escape. St Mary's.

Tanacetum vulgare **Tansy**
Rare. Bryher, St Mary's and St Agnes.

Seriphidium maritimum **Sea wormwood**
Rare. St Martin's and St Agnes.

Artemisia vulgaris **Mugwort**
Occasional. Bryher and St Mary's.

Artemisia absinthium **Wormwood**
Rare. St Mary's, St Martin's.

Santolina chamaecyparissus **Lavender-cotton**
Garden escape. Scattered records from the inhabited islands except Bryher.

Otanthus maritimus **Cottonweed**
Extinct.

Achillea millefolium **Yarrow**
Abundant. All the inhabited islands, also Samson, Northwethel and the Eastern Isles.

Chamaemelum nobile **Chamomile**
Locally frequent. A feature of coastal and heath grasslands on all inhabited islands.

Anthemis punctata **Sicilian chamomile**
Garden escape. St Martin's.

Anthemis arvensis **Corn chamomile**
Extinct? No recent records, formerly St Mary's.

Anthemis cotula **Stinking chamomile**
 Extinct?   Formerly St Mary's, St Agnes, Bryher.

Chrysanthemum segetum **Corn marigold**
Locally frequent/ abundant. All inhabited islands, especially St Mary's and St Agnes.

Leucanthemum vulgare **Oxeye daisy**
Rare/ occasional. Bryher and St Mary's. Plants on St Agnes came from a wildflower mix.

Matricaria recutita **Scented mayweed**
Occasional. Inhabited islands except Bryher.

Matricaria discoidea **Pineappleweed**
Locally abundant. Inhabited islands and Samson.

Tripleurospermum maritimum **Sea mayweed**
Locally frequent. Mainly coastal sites on most islands including larger uninhabited islands.

Tripleurospermum inodorum **Scentless mayweed**
Occasional. Inhabited islands except St Martin's.

Cotula australis **Annual buttonweed**
Garden escape? Tresco and St Mary's.

Senecio cineraria **Silver ragwort**
Garden escape. Bryher, Tresco, formerly St Mary's.

Senecio glastifolius **Woad-leaved ragwort**
Garden escape. Tresco and St Mary's.

Senecio grandiflorus **Purple ragwort**
Garden escape. Porth Mellon, St Mary's, possibly still there.

Senecio jacobaea **Common ragwort**
Locally frequent. All inhabited islands, also Annet, Samson, Teän and Eastern Isles. Attempts are being made to eliminate the plant where stock is grazed.

Senecio squalidus **Oxford ragwort**
Rare. Only recorded as a casual, from St Mary's and Teän .

Senecio vulgaris **Groundsel**
Locally abundant. All inhabited islands, plus Annet, Samson and Teän .

Senecio sylvaticus **Heath groundsel**
Locally frequent. Found on all the inhabited islands, plus Annet, Teän, smaller Eastern Isles and formerly Samson.

Senecio viscosus **Sticky groundsel**
Recorded in error? Usually is *S. sylvaticus* which is also sticky.

Pericallis hybrida **Cineraria**
Garden escape. Established in churchyards and around habitations on St Mary's, St Martin's and Tresco.

Delairea odorata **German-ivy**
Garden escape. Established on St Agnes, Tresco and St Mary's often near coast.

Brachyglottis repanda **Hedge ragwort**
Planted tree. Recorded from the inhabited islands.
Two other *Brachyglottis* have also been recorded although no evidence that any have become naturalised. These include *Brachyglottis* 'Sunshine' and *B. monroi* Monro's ragwort.

Tussilago farfar **Coltsfoot**
Rare. Only known from one site in Hugh Town, St Mary's.

Petasites fragans **Winter heliotrope**
Locally frequent. Scattered localities on all inhabited islands except St Martin's.

Calendula officinalis **Pot marigold**
Garden escape. A few localities on the inhabited islands except St Agnes, also recorded as casual from Samson.

Calendula arvensis **Field marigold**
Rare. Only known from a few fields on St Mary's.

Ambrosia artemisiifolia **Ragweed**
Birdseed annual. One record, Hugh Town, St Mary's.

Helianthus annuus **Sunflower**
Garden escape. St Mary's.

Helianthus petiolaris **Lesser sunflower**
Garden escape. Tresco.

Helianthus x *multiflorus* **Thin-leaved sunflower**
Garden escape. St Mary's.

Helianthus x *laetiflorus* **Perennial sunflower**
Garden escape. St Mary's.

Galinsoga quadriradiata **Shaggy-soldier**
Rare. Tresco and St Mary's in arable fields.

Bidens tripartita **Trifid bur-marigold**
Rare. Wetland areas, Tresco.

Eupatorium cannabidium **Hemp Agrimony**
Rare. As casual, Longstone Centre, St Mary's, probably introduced with
plants from the mainland. Formerly introduced with garden material St Agnes
but did not persist.

Ageratum houstonianum **Flossflower**
Garden escape. St Martin's.

Agapanthus praecox

LILIIDAE - MONOCOTYLEDONS

BUTOMACEAE

Baldellia ranculoides Lesser water-plantain
Rare. Wetland areas St Mary's. Not seen recently.

POTAMOGETONACEAE

Potamogeton natans Broad-leaved pondweed
Rare. Apparently extinct, formerly Lower Moors.

Potamogeton polygonifolius Bog pondweed
Rare. Lower Moors and Shooter's Pool area, St Mary's.

Potamogeton perfoliatus Perfoliate pondweed
Extinct.

Potamogeton pusillus **Lesser pondweed**
Extinct. Formerly pools Tresco and St Mary's.

Potamogeton pectinatus **Fennel pondweed**
Occasional. Most pools on the inhabited islands and Northwethel.

RUPPIACEAE

Ruppia maritima **Beaked tasselweed**
Rare. Pools on the inhabited islands, usually in brackish water.

ZOSTERACEAE

Zostera marina **Eelgrass**
Locally frequent. Shallow, sandy areas offshore.

ARACEAE

Zantedeschia aethiopica **Altar lily**
Escape from cultivation. All inhabited islands.

Arum italicum neglectum **Italian lord's and ladies**
Locally frequent. All inhabited islands and Samson.

Arum italicum italicum **Italian lord's and ladies**
Rare. St Mary's, probably garden escape.

LEMNACEAE

Lemna minor **Common duckweed**
Occasional. Wetlands St Mary's, Tresco and Bryher.

Lemna minuta **Least duckweed**
Locally frequent. Wetlands St Mary's, also found in water tank on Teän in 2002.

JUNCACEAE

Juncus gerardii **Saltmarsh rush**
Rare. Only from around pools Bryher and St Agnes.

Juncus bufonius **Toad rush**
Locally abundant. Found on all the inhabited islands and Samson. Found both in cultivated fields and wetlands.

Juncus articulatus **Jointed rush**
Occasional. St Mary's, Bryher and St Martin's.

Juncus acutiflorus **Sharp-flowered rush**
Rare. St Mary's.

Juncus bulbosus **Bulbous rush**
Rare. Scattered sites on St Mary's, St Martin's and St Agnes.

Juncus maritimus **Sea rush**
Locally frequent. Bryher, St Mary's, Tresco. The variety *atlanticus* is ascribed to the plants on St Mary's.

Juncus inflexus **Hard rush**
Rare. St Mary's and Tresco.

Juncus effusus **Soft rush**
Locally frequent. St Mary's and Tresco. The var *subglomeratus* has also been recorded.

Juncus conglomeratus **Compact rush**
Rare. Only recent record from near Porthellick, St Mary's in 1995.

Luzula campestris **Field wood-rush**
Locally frequent. All inhabited islands, Samson, St Helen's, Teän and Great Ganilly.

Luzula multiflora **Heath wood-rush**
Rare. A few sites Tresco and St Mary's.

CYPERACEAE

Eriophorum angustifolia **Common cottongrass**
Rare. Last recorded in Higher Moors, St Mary's in 1998.

Eleocharis palustris **Common spikerush**
Occasional. Scattered wetland sites on all the inhabited islands and Samson.

Eleocharis uniglumis **Slender spikerush**
Rare. Wetland sites Tresco, St Mary's and St Agnes.

Eleocharis multicaulis **Many-stalked spikerush**
Rare. Tresco, St Mary's and St Agnes.

Bolboschoenus maritimus **Sea club-rush**
Occasional. Wetland sites on the inhabited islands other than St Martin's, also in freshwater seepages on Annet.

Isolepis setacea **Bristle club-rush**
Occasional. Wet sites on inhabited islands other than Bryher. There may be some confusion between this species and *I. cernua.*

Isolepis cernua **Slender club-rush**
Rare. Tresco, St Mary's and St Agnes.

Carex paniculata **Greater tussock sedge**
Rare. Higher and Lower Moors, St Mary's. The tussocks at Higher Moors are impressively large.

Carex otrubae **False fox sedge**
Rare. St Mary's.

Carex muricata ssp *lamprocarpa* **Prickly sedge**
Probably extinct. Formerly Tresco.

Carex divulsa **Grey sedge**
Rare. Tresco and St Mary's.

Carex arenaria **Sand sedge**
Locally abundant. All inhabited and uninhabited islands other than small rocky ones. Occurs in habitats away from coast including heathland and wall-tops.

Carex remota **Remote sedge**
Rare. Abbey Wood, Tresco and St Mary's.

Carex echinata **Star sedge**
Extinct?   Formerly St Mary's.

Carex riparia **Greater pond sedge**
Rare. Tresco and St Mary's.

Carex pendula **Pendulous sedge**
Occasional. Tresco, St Mary's and St Martin's.

Carex sylvatica **Wood sedge**
Rare. Tresco Wood and Higher Moors area St Mary's.

Carex panicea **Carnation sedge**
Extinct?   Formerly St Mary's.

Carex laevigata **Smooth-stalked sedge**
Rare. St Mary's.

Carex binervis **Green-ribbed sedge**
Occasional. Mostly coastal heath, St Mary's.

Carex viridula oedocarpa **Yellow sedge**
Rare. Bryher, St Agnes and St Mary's.

Carex pilulifera **Pill sedge**
Occasional. Tresco, St Mary's and Gugh.

Carex nigra **Common sedge**
Extinct?

POACEAE

Pseudosasa japonica **Arrow bamboo**
Garden escape. Very rare St Mary's - including Toll's Island.

Festuca arundinacea **Tall fescue**
Rare. Only recorded from a field on Bryher.

Festuca rubra **Red fescue**
Abundant/locally dominant. Occurs on all the inhabited and most uninhabited islands. A variable grass, the subsp *juncea* has been recorded.

Festuca ovina **Sheep's fescue**
Occasional. All inhabited islands and Samson. Probably under-recorded.

Lolium perenne **Perennial rye-grass**
Abundant. All inhabited islands and Samson.

Lolium multiflorum **Italian rye-grass**
Occasional. All inhabited islands except Tresco.

Vulpia bromoides **Squirreltail fescue**
Abundant to occasional. All inhabited islands and Samson.

Vulpia myuros **Rat's-tail fescue**
Occasional. Inhabited islands other than Tresco.

Vulpia fasciculata **Dune fescue**
Rare. A record from dunes on Samson in 2007 needs confirmation.

Cynosurus cristatus **Crested dog's-tail**
Locally frequent. On all the inhabited islands. Formerly recorded on St Helen's.

Cynosurus echinatus **Rough dog's-tail**
Rare. St Mary's. Mostly recorded from Buzza Hill.

Puccinellia maritima **Common saltmarsh-grass**
Rare. Beside Bryher Pool and leat.

Briza minor **Lesser quaking-grass**
Locally abundant. In arable fields and disturbed ground on the inhabited islands.

Briza maxima **Greater quaking-grass**
Occasional. Found on a few sites on St Agnes, St Martin's and Tresco with most records from St Mary's.

Poa infirma **Early meadow-grass**
Locally frequent. Found mostly along pathways on all inhabited islands.

Poa annua **Annual meadow-grass**
Abundant. All inhabited islands, plus Samson and Norwethel.

Poa trivalis **Rough meadow-grass**
Locally frequent. Inhabited islands, also Samson (including Puffin Island), Northwethel, St Helen's and Teän.

Poa humilis **Spreading meadow-grass**
Occasional. Scattered records from the inhabited islands, Samson and formerly St Helen's.

Poa pratensis **Smooth meadow-grass**
Locally frequent. On the inhabited islands.

Dactylis glomerata **Cock's-foot**
Abundant. All inhabited and most uninhabited islands.

Catapodium rigidum **Ferngrass**
Occasional. All the inhabited islands. The var *majus* has been recorded from Abbey Gardens, Tresco and Hugh Town, St Mary's.

Catapodium marinum **Sea ferngrass**
Locally frequent. All inhabited islands, St Helen's and Teän.

Glyceria fluitans **Floating sweet-grass**
Rare. Pools and wet places St Mary's.

Glyceria x pedicellata **Hybrid sweet-grass**
Rare. Wet field, St Mary's.

Glyceria declinata **Small sweet-grass**
Rare. Pools and wet areas, St Mary's.

Glyceria noata **Plicate sweet-grass**
Rare. Tresco 2008..

Arrhenatherum elatius **False oatgrass**
Locally frequent. The inhabited islands, plus Samson, St Helen's, Northwethel, Teän and Little Arthur. The var *bulbosus* onion couch has been recorded from many islands and is probably the usual variety in Scilly.

Avena fatua **Wild-oat**
Rare. Scattered records from St Martin's, St Agnes and St Mary's.

Avena sativa **Oat**
Rare. Only recorded from Tresco and St Martin's.

Trisetum flavescens **Yellow oat-grass**
Possibly extinct. Formerly known only from Teän.

Koeleria macrantha **Crested hair-grass**
Rare. Scattered records from Bryher, Tresco and St Agnes.

Rostraria cristata
Extinct. Recorded from bulb-field on Tresco in 1957 but apparently did not persist.

Holcus lanatus **Yorkshire fog**
Abundant/ locally dominant. All inhabited and uninhabited islands save the Norrads and Western Rocks.

Holcus mollis **Creeping soft-grass**
Occasional. Scattered records from inhabited islands except St Agnes.

Aira caryophyllea Silvery hair-grass
Frequent. A common grass in many habitats. The plants on heathland and coastal habitats tend to be very small compared with those growing in arable habitats. The ssp *multiculmis* has been recorded from bulb fields on St Agnes, St Mary's and St Martin's.

Aira praecox Early hair-grass
Frequent. A common grass in many habitats. Heathland and coastal plants also tend to be small compared with those growing in arable habitats.

Anthoxanthemum odoratum Sweet vernal-grass
Frequent. Found on all the inhabited and many uninhabited islands.

Phalaris arundinacea Reed canary-grass
Rare. Only recorded from Lower Moors, St Mary's.

Phalaris canariensis Canary-grass
Rare. Casual, St Mary's.

Phalaris minor Lesser canary-grass
Rare. Casual on St Mary's. May have been more common formerly.

Agrostis capillaris Common bent
Abundant. Occurs on grassland, heathland and farmland, also in some arable fields on all the inhabited islands. Also recorded from Teän, St Helen's and Samson, but apparently absent from the Eastern Isles.

Agrostis gigantea Black bent
Rare. An uncommon grass in Scilly, found mostly from arable fields on Tresco and St Mary's.

Agrostis stolonifera Creeping bent
Abundant. A very common grass on both inhabited and uninhabited islands.

Agrostis canina **Velvet bent**
Occasional. According to Lousley this was a common grass on marshy
meadows on St Mary's. It has been recorded recently from wet grassland on
St Mary's, also from Tresco, and Samson, but it appears to be only locally
common. There may have been some confusion in the past with Brown Bent
Agrostis vinealis which is more often found in bulb fields and dry habitats.

Agrostis vinealis **Brown bent**
Occasional. Probably under-recorded due to confusion with *A. canina*. Occurs
on heathland and arable fields, in drier habitats than *A. canina*. Recorded on St
Agnes, Gugh, Bryher, Tresco and St Mary's.

Calamagrostis epigejos **Wood small-reed**
Occasional. Only found in the north east part of the archipelago. Is most
common on the uninhabited Eastern Isles, Teän and St Helen's, with a few
records from St Martin's and the north of St Mary's.

Ammophila arenaria **Marram**
Locally dominant. Both planted and native, it is a characteristic species of
sand dunes on both inhabited and uninhabited islands.

Gastridium ventricosum **Nitgrass**
Extinct? A record from1922 was accepted by Lousley but there have been no
records since.

Lagurus ovatus **Hare's-tail**
Rare. Casual recorded in Hugh Town in 1997.

Polypogon monspeliensis **Annual beard-grass**
Rare. Casual St Mary's.

Polypogon viridus **Water bent**
Rare. Only recorded from Shipman Head, Bryher.

Alopecurus pratensis **Meadow foxtail**
Rare. Only known from St Mary's.

Alopecurus geniculatus **Marsh foxtail**
Occasional. Only found in a few areas of wet grassland on Tresco, St Martin's and St Mary's.

Phleum pratense **Timothy**
Rare. Only two records, one from St Mary's and one from St Martin's.

Phleum bertolonii **Smaller cat's-ear**
Rare. Only record from wall on the Garrison, St Mary's.

Bromus commutatus x racemosus
Rare. One record from a bulb field on St Mary's.

Bromus hordeaceus **Soft-brome**
Frequent. Recorded on all the inhabited islands and St Helen's.

Bromus x pseudothominei **Lesser soft-brome**
Rare. One record from St Mary's.

Bromus secalinus **Rye brome**
Rare. Only known from a farm on St Mary's.

Anisantha diandra **Great brome**
Frequent. Found mostly in bulb and other arable fields on the inhabited islands.

Anisantha rigida **Ripgut brome**
Occasional. Recorded from bulb fields on St Agnes, St Martin's and St Mary's. There is a 1973 record from Bryher.

Anisantha sterilis **Sterile brome**
Locally frequent. Found on all the inhabited islands as well as a single record from Samson in 2000. There is some confusion with depauperate forms of *A. diandra*.

Anisantha madritensis **Compact brome**
Occasional. Recorded from bulb-fields on inhabited islands other than Tresco.

Ceratochloa cathartica **Rescue brome**
Occasional. Only known from bulb fields on St Martin's and St Mary's.

Brachypodium sylvaticum **False brome**
Abundant. Found in many habitats on all the inhabited and most uninhabited islands.

Elymus caninus **Bearded couch**
Rare. Only one (casual?) record from St Martin's in 1990.

Elytrigia repens **Common couch**
Occasional. Recorded on all the inhabited islands as well as Teän and the Arthur's. Plants of ssp *arenosa* have been recorded on Teän.

Elytrigia atherica **Sea couch**
Occasional. Scattered in dunes around the islands.

Elytrigia juncea **ssp** *boreoatlantica* **Sand couch**
Frequent. Dunes on inhabited islands and some uninhabited islands.

Leymus arenarius **Lyme grass**
Rare? Recorded from dunes St Mary's in 2007 and Samson 2008 . Possibly previously over-looked.

Hordeum murinum **Wall barley**
Rare. A very few records from St Martin's, Bryher and St Mary's.

Hordeum secalinum **Meadow barley**
Rare. Only recent record from St Martin's.

Danthonia decumbens **Heath-grass**
Locally frequent. Heathlands on all the inhabited islands, also St Helen's and Samson.

Cortaderia selloana **Pampas-grass**
Occasional. Established Appletree Banks and dunes on Tresco. Occasional garden escape St Mary's.

Molinia caerulea **Purple moor-grass**
Locally frequent. Heathland and wet grassland Tresco, St Mary's and St Martin's.

Phragmites australis **Reed**
Locally abundant. Associated with open water sites on St Mary's and Tresco. A prostrate reed grew in a bulb field on St Agnes.

Eragrostis cilianensis **Stink-grass**
Rare. Birdseed alien St Mary's.

Echinochloa crus-galli **Cockspur**
Rare. Casual in arable fields on St Mary's.

Setaria pumila **Yellow-grass**
Rare. Presumed birdseed alien, St Mary's.

Setaria verticillata **Rough bristle-grass**
Rare. Presumed birdseed alien, St Mary's.

Setaria viridus **Green bristle-grass**
Rare. Birdseed alien St Mary's.

Digitaria sanguinalis **Hairy finger-grass**
Rare. Birdseed alien from two different sites St Mary's.

Digitaria ciliaris **Tropical finger-grass**
Rare. Birdseed alien St Mary's.

Sorghum bicolor **Great millet**
Rare. Birdseed alien St Mary's.

SPARGANIACEA

Sparganium erectum **Branched bur-reed**
Extinct? Not recorded for over twenty years. Formerly Lower Moors and pond near Porthloo.

TYPHACEAE

Typa latifolia Greater reedmace/Bulrush
Locally frequent. Great Pool, Tresco, Higher Moors, St Mary's and Little
Pool, Bryher (a recent introduction?).

BROMELIACEAE

Fasicularia bicolor Rhodostachys
Occasional. Frequently planted and also naturalised in a few places notably in
the dunes on Tresco.

Ochagavia carnea Tresco rhodostachys
Rare. Naturalised in dunes on Tresco.

LILIACEAE

Kniphofia uvaria Red-hot-poker
Occasional. Naturalised on Tresco and St Mary's.

Kniphofia x praecox Greater red-hot-poker
Occasional. Naturalised on Tresco and Bryher.

Ornithogalum angustifolium Star-of-Bethlehem
Occasional. Recorded from St Agnes, St Mary's and St Martin's, usually in
bulb fields. May have been accidentally introduced with other bulbs.

[*Ornithogalum umbellatum* Star-of-Bethlehem]
The one record of this species needs confirmation due to possible confusion
with *O. angustifolium.*

Scilla verna Spring squill
Locally frequent. Mainly on west and south coasts of Bryher, with smaller
colonies on north-east coast of St Mary's and on Peninnis Head. Records from
Tresco and White Island, St Martin's need confirmation.

Scilla peruviana Portuguese squill
Garden escape St Mary's. Also cultivated as a crop.

Hyacinthoides non-scripta **Bluebell**
Locally abundant. Found on heathy areas on all the inhabited and larger uninhabited islands.

Hyacinthoides x *massartiana* **Hybrid bluebell**
Locally abundant. Mainly found in bulb-fields and cultivated areas on the inhabited islands where both parents occur.

Hyacinthoides hispanica **Spanish bluebell**
Occasional/locally frequent. Formerly cultivated, is found on all the inhabited islands and Samson but especially common on St Mary's.

Muscari comosum **Tassel hyacinth**
Rare. One record from St Martin's, a probable garden escape.

Allium roseum **Rosy garlic**
Locally frequent. St Martin's and St Mary's.

Allium neapolitanum **Neapolitan garlic**
Rare. St Martin's and St Mary's.

Allium triquetrum **Three-corned garlic**
Abundant. All inhabited islands plus a recent record from Samson.

Allium ampeloprasum var. babingtonii **Babington's leek**
Frequent. Has fluctuated in abundance, but still found on all the inhabited islands, although less common St Agnes and Bryher.

Allium ampeloprasum var. ampeloprasum **Wild leek**
Rare. Probably overlooked as not recorded until about 1991. Occurs in two places on the Garrison, St Mary's.

Allium neapolitanum **Neapolitanum garlic**
Rare. Tends to be an overlooked and not very frequent relic of cultivation on St Mary's and St Martin's.

Allium vineale **Wild/Crow garlic**
Rare. St Martin's and St Mary's.

Nothoscordum borbonicum **Honey bells**
Occasional. Scattered records around the inhabited islands except St Agnes.
May be speading.

Agapanthus praecox **African lily/Agapanthus**
subsp. orientalis
Frequent. Escape from cultivation now well established on St Agnes, St
Mary's and Tresco. The rhizomes are freely available and often thrown out
from gardens when the clumps have become too dense. The plants on
Appletree Banks, Tresco have been present since c1939.

Tristagma uniflorum **Spring starflower**
Rare. Garden escape and bulb field weed St Mary's & St Agnes.

Amaryllis belladonna **Jersey lily/Naked ladies**
Rare. Occasional escape from cultivation Tresco, St Mary's and St Martin's

Nerine sarniensis **Guernsey lily**
Occasional garden escape?

Leucojum vernum **Spring snowflake**
Rare. Garden escape Tresco & St Agnes.

Narcissus ssp.
Frequent. Many different varieties of cultivated narcissus have become
naturalised on all the inhabited islands.

Ruscus aculeatus **Butcher's broom**
Rare. Almost all plants occur on the Eastern Isles and the east end of St
Martin's. Plants on St Mary's may be of garden origin.

IRIDACEAE

Libertia formosa **Chilean-iris**
Rare. Garden escape naturalised in a few places on St Mary's and Tresco.

Sisyrinchium californicum
Rare. Naturalised in dunes on Tresco but not seen recently.

Aristea ecklonii **Blue corn-lily**
Occasional. Escape from cultivation Tresco and St Mary's.

Iris pseudacorus **Yellow iris/Flag iris**
Locally frequent. Wet fields, pools and the 'Moors' on Tresco and St Mary's.
A patch of yellow iris near the ruined cottages on Samson may be this species.

Iris foetisissima **Stinking iris**
Locally abundant. Found on all the inhabited islands also on Samson and
Teän.

Iris latifolia **English iris**
Rare. Garden escape St Mary's.

Iris x *xiphium* **Spanish iris**
Rare. Relict of cultivation or garden escape on St Martins and St Mary's.

Iris x *hollandica* **Dutch iris**
Rare. Relict of cultivation on St Martin's.

Watsonia borbonica **Bugle-lily**
Occasional. Escape from cultivation mainly on Tresco & St Mary's.

Gladiosus communis byzantinus **Whistling jacks**
Locally abundant. A relict of cultivation that is well established in bulb fields
and waste ground on the inhabited islands.

Ixia campanulata **Red corn-lily**
Occasional. Relic of cultivation on St Martin's and St Mary's.

Ixia paniculata **Tubular corn-lily**
Occasional. Relic of cultivation on St Martin's and St Mary's.

Sparaxis grandiflora **Plain harlequinflower**
Occasional. Relic of cultivation on St Martin's, St Mary's and St Agnes.

Freesia x hybrida **Freesia**
Rare. Relic of cultivation on Tresco and St Mary's.

Crocosmia x crocosmiifloa **Montbretia**
Locally frequent. Occurs on the inhabited islands especially along
hedgebanks. Apparently absent from Bryher.

Chasmanthe bicolor **Chasmanthe**
Occasional. Garden escape found on the inhabited islands other than Bryher.

AGAVACEAE

Agave americana **Century-plant**
Other than plants in Tresco Abbey Gardens there are a few agaves growing on
walls and informal gardens. None appear to be naturalised but have been
planted.

Cordyline australis **Cabbage-palm**
Rare. Although planted trees occur over all the inhabited islands, naturalised
seedlings are uncommon.

Phormium tenax **New Zealand flax**
Frequent. Although naturalised plants are found on the inhabited islands most
are planted.

Phormium cookianum **Lesser New Zealand flax**
Rare (except on St Martin's). Very occasionally planted. Naturalised plants of
this species are spreading in the Great Bay area of St Martin's where the Isles
of Scilly Wildlife Trust are making attempts to control them.

PONTEDERIACEAE

Pontederia cordata **Pickerel weed**
Planted in Abbey Pool, Tresco.

ORCHIDACEAE

Spiralis spiranthes Autumn lady's-tresses
Locally frequent. Found on short grassland on heathlands, dunes, cricket fields, around ancient monuments even lawns on all the inhabited islands. This orchid has 'good' years with hundreds of flowering spikes and other years with fewer plants flowering.

Anacamptis pyramidalis Pyramidal orchid
Rare. Known only from the dunes on Samson since about 1986. Believed to have originated from blown seed.

Gymnadenia conopsea Fragrant orchid
Extinct? Recorded from St Martin's in 1971, apparently did not persist.

Dactylorhiza fuchsii Common spotted orchid
Extinct? Recorded from Tresco in 1969.

Dactylorhiza praetermissa Southern marsh orchid
Rare. Only found on Lower and Higher Moors, St Mary's. Formerly found elsewhere on St Mary's. A report from Samson in 1986 is now believed to have been an error for Pyramidal Orchid.

Spiranthus spiralis

INDEX

95

Anthemis punctata, 72
Anthoxanthemum odoratum, 84
Anthriscus caucalis, 51
Anthriscus sylvestris, 51
Aphanes arvensis, 37
Aphanes australis, 37
Apium graveolens, 52
Apium inundatum, 52
Apium nodiflorum, 52
Apple, 37
Apple mint, 59
Aptenia cordifolia, 14
Arabidopsis thaliana, 28
Arenaria serpyllifolia, 18
Argentine dock, 23
Argentine fleabane, 71
Aristea ecklonii, 92
Armeria maritima, 24
Armoracia rusticana, 29
Arrhenatherum elatius, 83
Arrow bamboo, 81
Artemisia absinthium, 72
Artemisia vulgaris, 72
Arum italicum italicum, 77
Arum italicum neglectum, 77
Ash, 61
Asplenium adiantum-nigrum, 5
Asplenium marinum, 5
Asplenium obovatum ssp lanceolatum,
    5
Asplenium ruta-muraria, 6
Asplenium trichomanes quadrivalens,
    6
Asplenium x sarniensis, 5
Aster lanceolatus, 70
Aster novi-belgii, 70
Aster x versicolor, 70
Athyrium filix-femina, 6
Atriplex glabriuscula, 16
Atriplex halimus, 16
Atriplex laciniata, 16
Atriplex prostrata, 16
Atriplex x gustafssoniana, 16

Australian blackwood, 38
Australian tree-fern, 5
Autumn hawkbit, 68
Autumn lady's-tresses, 94
Avena fatua, 83
Avena sativa, 83
Azolla filiculoides, 7
Babington's leek, 90
Babington's orache, 16
Baldellia ranculoides, 76
Ballota nigra meridionalis, 57
Balm, 58
Balm of Gilead', 27
Balm-leaved figwort, 62
Barbarea verna, 29
Barbarea vulgaris, 29
Beaked hawk's-beard, 69
Beaked tasselweed, 77
Bear's breech, 64
Bearded couch, 87
Beech, 13
Bell heather, 32
Bellis perennis, 71
Bergenia crassifolia, 35
Bermuda buttercup, 49
Berula erecta, 51
Beta vulgaris ssp maritima, 17
Beta vulgaris ssp vulgaris, 17
betony, 1
Betony, 57
Betula sp, 14
Bidens tripartita, 75
Bird's-foot, 38
Bird's-foot clover/ Birdsfoot
    fenugreek, 40
Bithynian vetch, 39
Biting stonecrop, 35
Bittersweet, 54
Black bent, 84
Black bindweed, 22
Black horehound, 57
Black medick, 40
Black mustard, 31

96

99

103

114

Solidago virgaurea

1 *Euphorbia paralias* Sea Spurge

2 *Beta maritima* Sea Beet

3 *Crithmum maritimum* Rock Samphire

4 *Armeria maritima* Thrift

5 *Crambe maritima* Sea kale

6 *Eryngium maritimum* Sea Holly

1 *Calluna vulgaris* Ling

2 Erica cinerea Bell Heather

3 *Ornithopus pinnatus* Orange Birdsfoot

4 *Lotus corniculatus* Birdsfoot Trefoil

5 *Ophioglossum azoricum*
Small Adderstongue Fern

6 *Solidago virgaurea* Goldenrod

1 *Allium babingtonii* Babington's Leek

2 *Allium triquetum* Three-cornered Leek

3 *Chrysanthemum segetum* Corn marigold

4 *Claytonia perfoliata* Spring Beauty

5 *Erodium moschatum* Musk Storksbill

6 *Filago vulgaris* Common Cudweed

MORE BULBFIELD PLANTS

1 *Fumaria capreolata*
White Ramping Fumitory

2 *Gladiolus byzantinus* Whistling Jacks

3 *Oxalis pes-caprea* Bermuda Buttercup

4 *Lavatera cretica* Smaller Tree-mallow

5 *Misopates orontium* Weasel Snout

6 *Hypericum humifusium*
Trailing St John's –wort

1 *Anacamptis pyramidalis*
Pyramidal Orchid

2 *Viola kitaibeliana* Dwarf Pansy

3 *Trifolium occidentale* Western Clover

4 *Galium verum* Ladys bedstraw

5 *Daucus carota* Wild carrot

6 *Tripleurospermum maritimum*
Sea mayweed

1 *Carex paniculata* Tussock Sedge

2 *Iris pseudocorus* Yellow Iris

3 *Lycopus europaeus* Gypsywort

4 *Lythrum salicaria* Purple Loosestrife

5 *Ranunculus baudotii*
Seaside Buttercup

6 *Oenanthe fistulosa*
Tubular Water-dropwort

1 *Asplenium obovatum*
Lanceolate Spleenwort

2 *Jasione montana* Sheeps-bit

3 *Ononis repens* Common Restharrow

4 *Spergularia rupicola* Rock Sea-spurrey

5 *Umbilicus rupestris*
Wall Pennywort

6 *Arum italicum neglectum*
Italian Lords & Ladies

1 *Lavatera arborea* Tree Mallow

2 *Iris foetisissima* Stinking Iris

3 *Ulex europaeus* Gorse

4 *Lonicera periclynum* Honeysuckle

5 *Orobanche minor*
Common Broomrape

6 *Digitalis purpurea* Foxglove

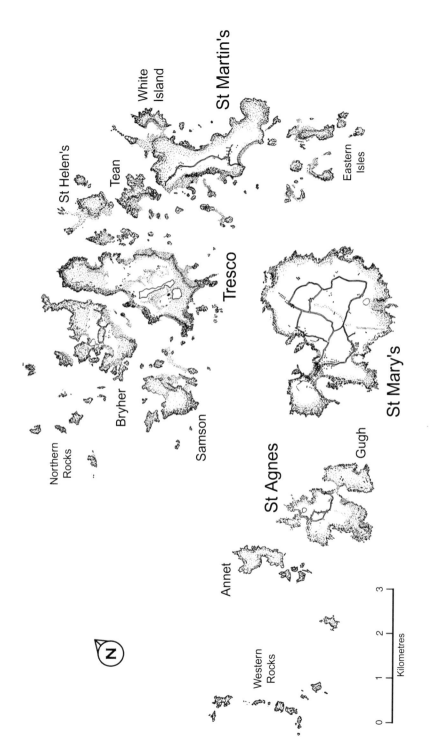

Map of the Isles of Scilly by Darren Rees

NOTES